Voices from the Mountains

OTHER BOOKS BY ANDREW D. MAYES

Celebrating the Christian Centuries (1999)

Spirituality of Struggle (2002)

Spirituality in Ministerial Formation (2009)

Holy Land? Challenging Questions (2011)

Beyond the Edge: spiritual transitions (2013)

Another Christ: re-envisioning ministry (2014)

Learning the Language of the Soul (2016)

Journey to the Centre of the Soul (2017)

Sensing the Divine (2019)

Gateways to the Divine: Transformative Pathways of Prayer from Jerusalem (2020)

Diving for Pearls: Exploring the Depths of Prayer with Isaac the Syrian (2021)

Voices from the Mountains

Forgotten Wisdom for a Hurting
World from the Biblical Peaks

ANDREW D. MAYES

WIPF & STOCK · Eugene, Oregon

VOICES FROM THE MOUNTAINS
Forgotten Wisdom for a Hurting World from the Biblical Peaks

Copyright © 2021 Andrew D. Mayes. All rights reserved. Except for brief quotations in critical publications or reviews, no part of this book may be reproduced in any manner without prior written permission from the publisher. Write: Permissions, Wipf and Stock Publishers, 199 W. 8th Ave., Suite 3, Eugene, OR 97401.

Wipf & Stock
An Imprint of Wipf and Stock Publishers
199 W. 8th Ave., Suite 3
Eugene, OR 97401

www.wipfandstock.com

PAPERBACK ISBN: 978-1-6667-1772-3
HARDCOVER ISBN: 978-1-6667-1773-0
EBOOK ISBN: 978-1-6667-1774-7

10/13/21

COPYRIGHT PERMISSIONS AND OTHER ACKNOWLEDGMENTS

Unless otherwise acknowledged, Scripture quotations are from New Revised Standard Version Bible, copyright © 1989, 1995 National Council of the Churches of Christ in the United States of America. Used by permission. All rights reserved worldwide.

Authorized (King James) Version (AKJV) reproduced by permission of Cambridge University Press, the Crown's patentee in the UK.

Easy-to-Read Version (ERV) Copyright © 2006 by Bible League International

Good News Translation (GNT) Copyright © 1992 by American Bible Society.

God's Word Translation (GW) Copyright © 1995, 2003, 2013, 2014, 2019, 2020 by God's Word to the Nations Mission Society. All rights reserved.

Revised Standard Version (RSV), copyright © 1946, 1952, and 1971 National Council of the Churches of Christ in the United States of America. Used by permission. All rights reserved worldwide

The Voice Bible (VOICE), Copyright © 2012 Thomas Nelson, Inc. The Voice™ translation © 2012 Ecclesia Bible Society All rights reserved.

Extracts from Jerome. *Commentary on Matthew*. Translated by Thomas P. Scheck. (Washington DC: Catholic University of America Press, 2008).

Extracts from Thomas J. Samuelian, trans., *Speaking with God from the Depths of the Heart* (Yerevan, Armenia: Vem, 2001). www.stgregoryofnarek.am/.

Extract from Yehuda Halevi, "Zion, Do You Wonder" in Hillel Halkin, trans., *Yehuda Halevi* (New York: Schocken Books, 2010).

Extracts from "The Rule of St Albert" translated by Bede Edwards ODC in Elizabeth Ruth Obbard, *Land of Carmel* (Gracewing, Leominster, 1999).

Extracts from Charles Upton, trans., *Doorkeeper of the Heart: Versions of Rabi'a* (New York: Pir, 1988).

Photo Credits:
1. wikipedia commons
2. sacredsites.com
3. israel-in-photos.com
4. pxfuel.com
5. author
6. author
7. wikipedia commons
8. wikipedia commons
9. author

Contents

Photographs | viii
Introduction | ix

1. Ararat—*Rediscovering God in Turbulent Times* | 1
2. Sinai—*Encountering the Divine in Darkness and in Light* | 18
3. Carmel—*Forging Prophets and Mystics* | 36
4. Zion—*Longing for Fulfilment* | 56
5. Desert Mountains—*Exploring the Terrain of Prayer* | 78
6. Galilean Mountains—*Inspiring a Unifying Vision* | 97
7. Tabor—*Transforming Perception* | 117
8. Olivet—*Building Hopefulness* | 133
9. Calvary—*Resourcing Courage* | 150

Conclusion | 164
Bibliography | 171

Photographs

1. Mount Ararat | xvi
2. Mount Sinai | 17
3. Mount Carmel | 35
4. Mount Zion | 55
5. Desert Mountains | 77
6. Galilean Mountains | 96
7. Mount Tabor | 116
8. Mount Olivet | 132
9. Mount Calvary | 149

Introduction

THE BIBLICAL MOUNTAINS LOOM large in the religious imagination. While some are snow-capped and soar into the sky, and others are holy hills, all are of huge spiritual magnitude and significance. They are cosmic mountains that have witnessed seismic spiritual events foundational to the tradition. As archetypal, immovable symbols of faith they stand firm through the millennia as signposts to the Divine. Genesis calls them "eternal mountains . . . everlasting hills" (49:26). In the shifting sands of today's uncertain world, where traditional paradigms are fragmenting and everything seems in a state of flux, they endure as unshakable and steadfast. Today as old familiar landmarks are passing and we find ourselves out of our comfort zone, we echo the pilgrim prayer of old: "I lift up mine eyes to the hills. From whence cometh my help?" (Ps 121, AKJV). Not only in the Scriptures but also in human experience through the centuries, the mountains have proved to be the locus of the Divine where a sense of God's presence has been tangibly, palpably felt. They are places where an often enigmatic and elusive God makes theophany, revelation: an axis and intersection between heaven and earth, divine-human nexus. They are places set apart.[1]

Because the mountains are so central to the biblical narrative, we can become de-sensitized to their wonder and abiding messages, as we may be

---

1. Behind the word "holy" the root meaning of the Hebrew *qadesh* is to separate, to set apart.

Introduction

familiar, or over-familiar, with the narratives in the Scriptures. Yet in their caves and canyons linger ancient voices that can startle us into new insight and awaken in us new ways of seeing the world and ourselves. In this book we go on a quest to locate the ancient voices of those who actually lived in the mountains, and who long pondered their mysteries. Some whisper to us from the depths of hidden crevices; some boom from the summits, ricocheting across the ravines and across the centuries till they reach our ears, and hearts, today. We encounter people who actually lived there and who knew both the physical contours and spiritual secrets of the mountains. We will rediscover texts and fragments that have been long-forgotten in the West—maybe long out of print or otherwise tucked away in obscure or neglected corners, not easy to locate. This book makes these hidden resources accessible to the general reader.[2] We are summoned to begin a trek and spiritual adventure that will enable us to stumble on subversive wisdom —sometimes unnerving and at other times strangely re-assuring. We will never again see these mountains and their message in the same way.

We will find the mountains to be liminal spaces that can change our thinking in inspiring, unsettling and energizing ways. In entering liminal space, you leave behind your former ideals and conventions, the status quo, the ordinary routines, inherited mind-sets. You also leave behind your safety zone, you quit your place of security. You step out into a space where you will see things differently, where your world-view might be shattered, where your existing priorities might be turned upside down. You cross a border and go beyond your usual limits. What had been a barrier now becomes a threshold, a stepping stone into a larger spiritual adventure. The liminal spaces into which the mountains draw us are places of radical unmaking and unlearning—sometimes uncomfortable spaces where we're called to be utterly vulnerable to God, and from which we will re-enter the world quite changed, even converted! The *limen* is the threshold, the place of departure, a springboard into a fresh way of doing things . . .[3] In the liminal places of the mountains we might leave behind our existing mindset

---

2. Footnotes provide sources for further study and scholarly works.

3. The concept of liminality derives from van Gennep, *Rites de Passage*, 1909 anthropological study of ritual in communities. He identified three stages in a process of transition which resonate with the mountain imagery of ascent, summit and descent: *separation*, breaking with past practices and expectations; *liminal state* where those to be initiated, for example young people into adulthood, must face challenges to their sense of identity and a process of re-formation; *aggregation* or reintegration into the community as a changed person with a sharpened sense of values.

Introduction

and learn to perceive things afresh. We may, indeed, clarify our sense of identity, purpose and vocation. Things are discovered in the liminal zone that can't be found in the routines of normal life.[4]

So there is a paradox at the outset: the immovable mountains can reassure and hearten us, but their voices can also unsettle and challenge. The backdrop to the writing of this book is the coronavirus pandemic, which has filled the world with uncertainty and fear. We will discover wisdom and insights that are strikingly relevant to this unfolding world crisis and which speak with an uncanny directness to our situation. But the wisdom here is timeless and enduring, and readers will benefit from these ancient voices in all generations and in all sorts of circumstances. Right now we find ourselves in a liminal time—between two eras, neither one thing nor the other—when we find ourselves longing with nostalgia for old, familiar certainties and securities, for the "normal", for the traditional and safe. But we find, instead, that it is *precisely* in risky and unpredictable places that the Divine waits to meet us, to reveal himself to us. We find ourselves in a liminal zone that is, at the same time, not only bewildering and disorientating but also the place of discovery, creativity, potentiality. The place of risk is a place of paradox: it is discomforting but strangely renewing.

This book invites us to make the ascent into places—literal and metaphorical—that will be at once testing and revelatory. This book can help us reflect on our own discipleship and venturesomeness. Indeed the experience of prayer itself can be a liminal state, demanding of us that we let go of beliefs or ways of doing things that have got us into a rut, and beckoning us to fresh discoveries of God. In our personal lives and times of prayer we often find ourselves thirsting for something more, of which the peak of the mountains, the beckoning summit, may be a symbol. But what will we find when we get there? The voices we will listen to in this book will open before us fresh vistas, new panoramas, wider perspectives . . .

How, then, should we approach ancient texts that come from a distant age or thought world? Philip Sheldrake writes: "What is needed is a receptive and at the same time critical dialogue with a spiritual text in order to allow the wisdom contained in it to challenge us and yet to accord our own horizons their proper place."[5] We need both a hermeneutic of generosity,

---

4. Victor Turner, *Ritual Process* noticed that the transitional phase was a testing process of undoing and remaking. He explores pilgrimage as a liminal experience in Turner & Turner, *Image and Pilgrimage*.

5. Sheldrake, *Spirituality and History*, 165.

Introduction

honoring ancient voices, and also a hermeneutic of suspicion in which we feel free to bring forward our questions.[6] Indeed, in this dialogue, there is a two-way questioning: we allow ancient voices to question us, and we may bring our questions and puzzlements to the texts we encounter. Within this dialectic, who can predict how the mountains might change or transform us?

OUTLINE OF THIS BOOK

Each chapter opens with a vivid first-hand description by the author of the holy mount and some initial biblical reflections. Next we listen to the voices speaking to us. We will hear twenty voices of spiritual writers who lived on the mountains or made significant visits, and five voices of those who did not reach the mountains but pondered long and deep on their meaning and whose lives were dominated by such mounts. A section entitled "Questions for today" will begin to open up a dialogue, as our context and its extraordinary demands seek to learn from ancient sources of wisdom. Finally, each chapter offers the reader a section "For personal reflection", challenges to stimulate individual response and appropriation of the material: these can also be used in groups. This book is not so much an anthology of forgotten voices as a sourcebook of spirituality and a guidebook for the spiritual adventure.

We begin with the archetypal tale of the Great Flood as we ponder the message of the stunning mountain of Ararat. As we listen to the voices of Armenian mystics Gregory of Narek (tenth century) and Nerses Shnorhali (twelfth century), we revisit our understanding of the vocation of the church in turbulent times and reflect on our image of God. Chapter 2 takes us to Sinai—where we are invited to find God both in the deep darkness of unknowability and in dazzling light of revelation. Our guides on this primordial mountain will be Gregory of Nyssa's *Life of Moses* (fourth century) and those who lived for many years on the holy mountain itself in the seventh and eight centuries: John Climacus, Hesychios of Sinai and Philotheos of Sinai.

Next Elijah beckons us up to the crest of Mount Carmel. We ponder the message of his life and listen to the voices of St Albert (thirteenth century), and the great Carmelite John of the Cross (sixteenth century) who offers us a view of the spiritual adventure in his classic *The Ascent of Mount*

6. See Miles, *Image and Practice*, x.

Introduction

Carmel. We ponder the interplay between action and contemplation, between the prophetic and mystical dimensions of discipleship. We also address the issue of stress.

Mount Zion becomes the focus of humanity's deepest longing in chapter 4. We listen to the voices of Mount Zion as we see how people's ache for God, our insatiable spiritual desire, the craving of the soul becomes concentrated with intensity on one holy mountain. Because Zion is of special significance to all three monotheistic religions, in this longer chapter we will hear two voices from each tradition: Jewish cries for Zion, expressed by Moses Maimonides and Yehuda Halevi (twelfth century), the Muslim longings of remarkable woman mystic Raba'a (eighth century) and Al-Ghazali (eleventh century) and Christian aspirations uttered by Sophronius (seventh century) and Bernard of Clairvaux (twelfth century).

Next we venture into the mountains of the Judean desert. Amidst the rocks and canyons we catch the whisper of the very first monks Chariton and Euthymius (fourth century), and we find, perhaps surprisingly, that their cries resonate powerfully with contemporary concerns, not least with the tensions we face between the polarities of solitude and hospitality, stability and upheaval, stillness and movement. Basil the Great (fourth century), who learnt much in this liminal desert landscape, communicates to us his vision of a life of prayer.

Trekking to the Sea of Galilee in chapter 6, and following the itinerary offered us in Matthew's gospel, we encounter four mountains: the mountain of teaching (Mount Beatitudes), the mount of healing and feeding, the mountain of the Great Commission and the "Other Side" (Golan Heights). Jerome (fourth century), a frequent visitor here, will be our guide as we seek today a unifying vision in a world marked by division and fragmentation.

Ascending Mount Tabor we must be prepared to have our perceptions transformed and learn to see things quite differently within the divine light. Gregory Palamas (fourteenth century) opens to us the dazzling mysteries, not only of Christ's transfiguration but also of our human potential for deification.

On the Mount of Olives, where in the gospels Martha and Mary speak so powerfully, we are challenged by two remarkable women Melania the Elder and her grand-daughter sharing the same name (fourth century). We are awed by their capacity to make things happen, by their vision and infectious, indefatigable hopefulness. We hear too from their friend, the

Introduction

great theologian Rufinus who lived on the sacred mount at this time in the fourth/fifth centuries and from the Elder's protégé Evagrius.

As we approach the sacred hill of Calvary, we find ourselves in good company. Cyril of Jerusalem (fourth century) shares his teaching with us while Hesychius of Jerusalem (fifth century) beckons us to new courage and steadfastness in the face of trials.

The book's conclusion becomes a springboard into the future as we hear Gregory of Nyssa challenge us to keep on and on in our spiritual quest and in an untiring ascent of mountains of prayer and revelation.

Conditioned by the limitations of their time, many centuries considered the mountains too risky a place for women to dwell alone, and there is a regrettable shortage of women's voices to be heard. Certainly, the awesome insights of Raba'a on Zion and the two Melanias on Olivet go some way to correct this imbalance. The voice of intrepid Spanish pilgrim Egeria (fourth century) will guide us at times. Readers may also have to bear in mind that many monks and mystics we encounter here were writing in the first instance for their brothers in community, so in places the masculine pronoun may predominate. However, extracts that are out of copyright have been reworked in favor of inclusive language, and the wisdom that comes to us from the mountains speaks powerfully to all genders.

OUR APPROACH TO THE MOUNTAINS

We approach the mountains with awe and respect—they are not to be conquered but encountered. We are keenly aware that we walk on sacred ground. Like Moses on Horeb we might, as it were, take off our shoes for we find ourselves treading on hallowed terrain, rock and earth made holy by the presence of the Divine and by the prayers of the centuries. We will not focus in this book on the ascent, except in one or two parts, but we remind ourselves, at the outset, that the path may be dangerous and risky. There are hazardous and slippery paths or diversions in the spiritual odyssey. But at the outset, we remind ourselves that determination and discipline are needed. All spiritual writers speak of the indispensability of spiritual disciplines like daily prayer, scripture reading, service to others, solitude, eucharist, self-examination and confession and for some, fasting.[7] Indeed, as we shall discover in the desert mountains, pioneers of spiritual life emphasized

---

7. See, for example, Foster, *Celebration of Discipline;* Willard, *Spirit of the Disciplines;* Whitney, *Spiritual Disciplines.*

Introduction

the need for *ascesis*, discipline or training, echoing Paul's reference to the Christian as an athlete (1 Cor 9:24–27). In other words, this is not a book to be read in isolation from the demands of Christian discipleship, though the uncommitted enquirer or seeker will indeed find much to enrich his or her spiritual quest.[8]

USING THIS BOOK

This book can be read on pilgrimage to the holy places. I well remember, when I was a young theological researcher living in Jerusalem, the joy and wonder of reading the text (albeit in English!) of Cyril of Jerusalem's *Catechetical Lectures* in the very place where they were delivered in 350—at the foot of Calvary and by the empty tomb, the *Anastasis*. There was an amazing sense of connection, of communion, indeed of continuity with the past as Cyril's words came alive once more in the present moment. But this book is designed mainly for those who do not plan a visit to the holy mountains themselves, but who long to enter into their sacred precincts and spaces in imagination and in prayerful, theological reflection—that might, perhaps, be life-changing! So let us in heart and mind prepare to make the ascent. Above all, let us ready ourselves to be able to listen to the Voices that address us, so we can hear what they are saying to today's world, and make our response . . .

---

8. As a precursor to this book I have explored the spirituality of descent and the imagery of underground in the Holy Land in Mayes, *Journey to the Centre of the Soul.*

1

Ararat

Rediscovering God in Turbulent Times

> *The waters gradually receded from the earth . . . the ark came to rest on the mountains of Ararat. The waters continued to abate . . . the tops of the mountains appeared. (Gen 8: 3–5)*

I GASPED WHEN I first saw it. It literally took my breath away. I just wasn't expecting it. I couldn't believe my eyes. On a flight from Sydney to London at 36000 feet I looked out of the plane's window not long after dawn. I recognized immediately its twin peaks making a perfect M shape, for it was strangely familiar. Having lived in Jerusalem with the Armenian community for a year—I was a research student at the Theological Seminary in the Old City—I discovered that the shape of Mount Ararat was ubiquitous because it had become a sort of logo or icon for the Armenian people. Indeed it is the central symbol on the national coat of arms. I had seen it in Jerusalem on posters and buildings in the Armenian Quarter so I recognized it instantly when I saw it with my own eyes, blinking in disbelief.

Looming above the plains of Eastern Anatolia, Ararat is certainly awesome, spectacular. Rising majestically to nearly 17000 feet, clouds clustered beneath it, even at a distance it radiated an aura, its snow-capped pinnacles shimmering in the early sunlight, penetrating azure heavens. In fact it is a volcano, last erupting in a major way in 1840 with an associated earthquake with a magnitude 7.4.

A month after that memorable flight in 2006, I was able to appreciate it from the ground, on a pilgrimage to Armenia, led by Bishop Geoffrey Rowell. The awesome white mount towered in the distance over the plain as we visited the monastery of Khor Virab ('deep prison'), where the evangelist of Armenia, Gregory the Illuminator, was incarcerated for thirteen years prior to his conversion of King Trdat III in 303AD—he went on to declare Armenia the first Christian nation in the world. For centuries Ararat was the treasured heart of the ancient Armenian homeland but in 1517 it was absorbed into the Ottoman Empire and now finds itself in south eastern Turkey, not far from the border with Iran. I recalled Noel Buxton's 1914 description of it:

> Ararat, flanked with sunset color, dominated the world below. Ararat is higher than Mount Blanc, and standing alone it towers uniquely. Yet there is something especially restful about its broad shoulders of perpetual snow. With the soaring quality of Fuji it combines a sense of holding, up there, a place of repose . . . It was a memorable combination—the eternal snow one associates with the north framed with the glowing brilliance of the southern sun.[1]

Armenians liken the snow-capped peak to a bride covering her head with a veil, and the distinctive pointed hats of Armenian priests are often said to remind the faithful of beloved Ararat. I understood why the story of Noah's Ark was so special to the Armenians, for the nation traces its origins to Noah's son Japheth, whose grandson was Hayk, father of the Armenian people (the original name for the country was Hayk; its contemporary native name is *Hayastan*). Genesis 9:26—10:2 tells us:

> Noah said: "Give praise to the LORD, the God of Shem! . . . May God cause Japheth to increase!". . . These are the descendants of Noah's sons, Shem, Ham, and Japheth. These three had sons after the flood. The sons of Japheth . . . were the ancestors of the peoples who bear their names. (GNT)

The Book of Genesis (8:4) identifies the "mountains of Ararat" as the resting place of Noah's Ark after the Great Flood described in its text. It is on these sacred slopes that God makes his awesome promise and opens a new Covenant with humanity and with all creation.

---

1. Noel and Harold Buxton *Travels and Politics in Armenia*. London 1914, quoted in Walker, *Visions of Ararat*, 108. The Harold Buxton Trust supported my visit to Armenia in 2006.

Ararat

GREGORY OF NAREK (945–1003)—hailed as the best representative of medieval Armenian spirituality and, indeed as one of the greatest Christian mystics of all time—lived in the shadow of Ararat, both physically and spiritually. This tenth-century author is little discovered outside the Armenian church—though his voice is beginning to be heard since Pope Francis declared him to be a Doctor of the Church in 2015. Gregory became abbot of the monastery on the shores of Lake Van in historic Armenia. From the hills above the monastery he could catch a glimpse of Ararat a hundred miles away. Considered the first poet of the Armenians, Gregory gathered together ninety-five stunning prayers in a work *Speaking with God from the Depths of the Heart* which he called an "encyclopedia of prayer for all nations", hoping it might be a guide to prayer for people around the world. The mountain looms in its significance:

> If I were to set the cedars of Lebanon as a scale
> and to put Mount Ararat on one side
> and my iniquities on the other,
> it would not come close to balancing.[2]

Such is the spirit of humility and penitence in which Gregory writes his prayers. His voice echoes across the centuries because

> In a tranquil period,
> when the enemies of the church were restrained,
> I undertook the writing of this book.
> I planned, arranged, compiled, and set it forth,
> bringing together in one comprehensive work,
> in a single style, passages from many different sources,
> to produce this sacred book.[3]

The tone is set in its opening words:

> The voice of a sighing heart, its sobs and mournful cries,
> I offer up to you, O Seer of Secrets,
> placing the fruits of my wavering mind
> as a savory sacrifice on the fire of my grieving soul
> to be delivered to you in the censer of my will.

---

2. Also known as *The Lamentations of Gregory of Narek*. Gregory of Narek (trans. Samuelian), *Speaking with God*, Prayer 9a, 37.

3. Gregory of Narek (trans. Samuelian), *Speaking with God*, Postscript, 470.

> Compassionate Lord, breathe in
> this offering and look more favorably on it
> than upon a more sumptuous sacrifice
> offered with rich smoke. Please find
> this simple string of words acceptable.
> Do not turn in disdain.
>
> May this unsolicited gift reach you,
> this sacrifice of words
> from the deep mystery-filled chamber
> of my feelings, consumed in flames
> fueled by whatever grace I may have within me . . .
> A new book of psalms sings with urgency through me,
> for all thinking people the world over,
> expressing all human passions
> and serving with its images
> as an encyclopedic companion to our human condition,
> for the entire, mixed congregation of the
> Church universal . . . [4]

As Gregory reflected on the story of Noah and the Great Flood, and the enduring message of Mount Ararat, three themes emerged:

1 Discerning a Call: the Church as a Place of Safety and Refuge

Gregory sees the message of Mount Ararat as being a call to the church to rediscover its vocation as an ark of salvation:

> The Church is an ark of purity,
> a second cause of rejoicing
> who saves us from drowning
> in the tumult of our worldly lives.
> She does not gather all sorts of beasts and just a few humans [like Noah's Ark]
> but rather gathers the heavenly host together with us mortals.
> She is not tossed about on waves of agitation,
> but rises above it to the heavenly heights.
> As a disciple under the command of the Holy Spirit of God
> she avoids iniquity.
> She does not demand a death blow to the flesh
> but rather guides those in her care

---

4. Gregory of Narek (trans. Samuelian), *Speaking with God*, Prayer 1a, 1.

to the good news of life.
She is not built by the hand of Noah,
but is built by the command of the creator.
She is not adorned by Moses with the craftsman Bezaleel [who decorated the Tabernacle]
but by the only begotten Son of God
    with the Holy Spirit.
She is not in perpetual motion, constantly changing,
but is established permanently upon an
unshakable foundation.
Like the ark made of wooden planks . . .
still she guides us anew.
In the image of the creator's infinite plenitude
she goes ahead to prepare for us a place in
the light of life.[5]

2 Making Sense of Suffering: Recovering Hope in a Time of Calamity

The tale of the Great Flood provides Gregory with a vocabulary and fountain of metaphors with which to make sense of his own suffering. The ark of his body has been sorely buffeted. His personal experience of fear and stress depicted in this imagery shifts to a sense of trust and hopefulness. As I recall from my visit in 2006, as we struggled to reach the island of Agthamar across chilly choppy waters, Lake Van where Gregory lived can quickly become turbulent and storm-tossed, a mirror of the soul:

> The ways of my life are like the waves of the sea,
> my soul tossing in this world upon countless, endless swells,
> riding in the shell of my body
> like the ship lost at sea . . .
> Wrecked by the blow of the wild waves of the sea, like a ship
> whose rudder has become unhinged,
> whose tall mask has been ripped from the deck,
> whose flapping sails are in shreds,
> whose well-built frame has lost its form,
> whose ropes have unravelled,
> whose lookout has been laid low,
> whose cable strands have snapped,
> whose anchor has come loose,

    5. Gregory of Narek (trans. Samuelian), *Speaking with God*, Prayer 75j, 347.

Voices from the Mountains

whose joints are unjointed,
whose guiding oar is bent,
whose keel is submerged,
whose helm is detached,
whose steering mechanism has gone,
whose backbone has snapped,
whose ribs are undone . . .
whose cabin has collapsed,
whose railing has fallen,
whose captain's chair has tipped,
whose deck planks have spilt apart,
whose fastening nails are out.

This image of destruction reminds me of my misery,
like a captain mourning his ship,
chin in hand, tears streaming down . . .
I did not stray from the truth
in selecting these words to mourn
the shattered ark of my intellect.
For the Good Captain with his heavenly host
took pity on the sea of humanity in just this way.

I wonder:
    Will I ever see the battered ark of my body restored?
    Will I ever see my shipwrecked soul healthy again? . . .
    Will I ever see the thousand cracks
in my vessel mended? . . .
But by your good will
    if the light of compassion should shine,
    if the door of your mercy should open,
    if the rays of your glory should spread . . .
    if the drops of your pure love should drop down . . .
then with this blessing
shall the faith of steady hope be forever mine
finding refuge in the Holy Spirit,
who with the Father is worshiped
with the voice of sweetness
and together with you [O Christ] bathed in light too bright
for human eyes . . .
Indeed, through you, O merciful Lord,
all things, in all ways, for all people, are possible.[6]

---

6. Gregory of Narek, *Speaking with God*, Prayer 25, a-d, 101–3. See also Prayer 54d, 242.

Ararat

Gregory feels vulnerability due to physical frailty and mental anguish and finds himself praying:

> If a violent storm suddenly strikes
> the vessel of the human body
> on its voyage through this world,
> steady its course with your rudder and
> send it sailing back toward you.[7]

> Jesus, accept with favor
> the supplications I make to you,
> and turn my gnawing apprehensions into solid faith.
> In the time of the Great Flood that destroyed everything,
> those who lived carelessly without fear
> upon the steady plains of earth
> were destroyed, bereft of your mercy,
> while those who trusted in your name,
> stood on the rocking deck
> of the covered ark of logs
> and were saved.
> Even so, rescue me with your love of mankind,
> though I forever sway this way and that, and
> deliver me to the port of your peace, I pray you.[8]

Confidence and hopefulness rise in Gregory's heart:

> You are my only hope of atonement, healing and salvation,
> redeemer of all mortals, renewer of the universe . . .
> . . . my wrongs are even greater than
> all the waters of seas in torrential flood,
> inundating and submerging the mountains.
> Release but a breath of your kindness
> as in Noah's day, a breath that can melt mountains,
> and the stormy flood of my billowing misdeeds
> will evaporate along with
> my earth-shattering transgressions
> and my mountain-high sins.[9]

---

7. Gregory of Narek, *Speaking with God,* Prayer 3d, 16.
8. Gregory of Narek, *Speaking with God,* Prayer 85b, 396.
9. Gregory of Narek, *Speaking with God,* Prayer 15c, 62.

3 Discovering a God of Mercy and Compassion

As Gregory reflects on the meaning of the Great Flood and the new beginning for creation made possible by the promise and covenant God made on the slopes of Ararat, he is overwhelmed by God's mercy which outweighs his judgement:

> You were not gratified by
> the destruction of the impious likes of me.
> Rather with melancholy tenderness,
> you are doubly aggrieved by the destruction
> of the iniquitous in the Flood,
> considering their death intolerable and repugnant,
> and saying in your heart the amazing words:
> "I shall never again curse the earth because of the
> deeds of men"
> And you were greatly consoled and rejoice in
> the deliverance of unclean men worthy of destruction . . .
> Sprinkle on me the dew of your compassionate
> fatherly love, living God, so that I too may find salvation through
> the pardoning of my sins
> by your abundant mercy.[10]

Gregory discovers God to be

> O totally generous God, whose patience never ends . . .
> You alone are the means of our salvation . . .
> Unending calm . . .
> calm for the troubled . . .
> rain of blessing . . .
> helmsman of the soul.[11]

God of Paradox

The story of Noah brims with paradox. The Flood is an ending and a beginning, destruction giving way to new life, a foretaste of the paschal mystery. Mount Ararat itself is an enigma: it seems to be an immovable mountain but erupts as an unpredictable volcano. So Gregory discovered paradox to be at the heart of his encounter with a God of judgment and mercy:

---

10. Gregory of Narek, *Speaking with God*, Prayer 60f, 268.
11. Gregory of Narek, *Speaking with God*, Prayer 32c, 143, 144.

> Lord God of all, able to do anything,
> all-encompassing space, unbounded, unlimited,
> close to all with your very essence,
> nowhere, yet without you there are no bounds,
> invisible, yet without the light of your dawn
>   nothing is visible,
> awesome glory, incomprehensible name,
>   voice of majesty, sound of the infinite,
>   essence beyond analysis,
> unreachable distance, immediate closeness,
> who notes gentleness and sees distress,
> stands by grief and can cure all hopeless cases,
> Father of compassion who spreads mercy,
>   God of comfort.[12]

Gregory identifies closely with Job, who moved from a sense of confusion about God, in the midst of his suffering, to a new perception of God's mystery:

> Like the path of blessed Job, I followed my
>   path of no return ...
> Like Job, I made my heavy yoke
>   even more intolerable ...
> For as Job said, the snares of evil are all around,
> from these I cannot escape ...
>   And like Job, I doubt you hear me ...[13]

Like Job he wrestles with the attempt to find meaning in suffering. Though he feels sinful unlike the innocent Job, he shares with him a keen sense of mortality and puzzlement. Like Job he comes to a fresh perspective on the paradoxes of the suffering and love, of divine presence and seeming absence, of judgement and mercy. Like Job Gregory comes to a place of surrender and acknowledgment of God's inscrutable ways:

---

12. Gregory of Narek, *Speaking with God*, Prayer 23a, 93.
13. Gregory of Narek, *Speaking with God*, Prayers 5e, 24; 20f, 84; 25e, 104; 28c, 121.

> You who chart the safe path on the sea
> between death and life, testifying that even
> in that perilous place we are protected through you ...
> You who shake the limitless density of the land
> like a small sailboat tossing on the waves,
> by which you put all creatures on notice
> that you are decisively in control,
> holding the whole world in your hand.[14]

The God Gregory discovers on the shore of Lake Van and in the shadow of Mount Ararat is not only a savior, but one who opens up new futures. God becomes for Gregory

> Glorified God in heaven,
> sole creator, lord of all,
> awesome majesty,
> compassion worthy of blessing ...
> you calm storms and restore tranquility to the waves,
> you hold the rudder of my impulsive will
> and taming it with your wisdom,
> you guide me back to you ...
> O Almighty,
>   you make it possible to reach the infinite heights.[15]

NERSES SHNORHALI (1102–1173)—his name means "grace-filled"—the outstanding Armenian Orthodox theologian, poet, composer, and historian—develops the hermeneutic approach of Gregory. As leader (Catholicos) of the Armenian Church he was deeply involved in attempts at ecumenical reconciliation with the Greek and Latin churches. He lived near Lake Kharput, some distance from Ararat, but in a sense he lives in the shadow of the holy mountain as he carefully ponders the message of the Flood. In his long poem *Jesus, Son Only Begotten of the Father* Nerses makes a personal reading of the parables and episodes of the Old Testament and gospel, locating himself as participant and recipient in the action, identifying himself with the characters. For him, it is experience and involvement and engagement with the sacred text that matters. His reflections on the Flood incorporate some startlingly fresh imagery:

---

14. Gregory of Narek, *Speaking with God*, Prayer 63c, 282.
15. Gregory of Narek, *Speaking with God*, Prayer 90a,b, 408, 410.

Ararat

And, as it fell in early days,
The days when Noah lived on earth,
They ate and drank and revel held
Until the floods of waters came
Destroying each and all of them
Save him who for five hundred years
Had lived a life of purity.

'Twas Noah and his family,
In number there were eight in all,
Who in the Ark were kept alive
Together with all kinds of beasts
And every kind of fowl as well.

Oh! Keep Thou me from floods of sin
And Satan's waves which drown my soul.
Within the shelter of Thine Ark
Of Covenant preserve me safe.

Remove from me the raven black
Which sees at night; He doth portray
The darts from ambush shot at night.

And open Thou in my dark heart
A window for the blessed Sun.
May sin-born clouds be driven from it
That they no more return to me.

Send through the open window-pane
The Holy Dove, the Golden One
Which is the Pure and Holy Ghost,
To bring to me the olive branch.

Not only did I drown myself
In fleshly lusts, but oft my heart
And mind were tools for Satan's use . . .
Deliver me from all the toils
Of sin in which I am enmeshed;
From diverse ills . . .
. . . like a pilgrim wandering,
My soul longs for the Heavenly Home.[16]

16. Shnorhali, *Jesus, Son Only Begotten*, 21–24.

He pictures his soul as an ark on "the waves of evil that agitate the world"[17], and observes

> It is not through bodily sickness
> That I drowned my soul in the sea,
> But through spiritual and mental torments.[18]

But he realizes that he is not a helpless victim but can take responsibility by opening wide the windows of his soul to the divine light and to the Dove of the Holy Spirit. He can welcome the Divine in the midst of the turbulence.

Seeking the Ark

JACOB OF NISIBIS (d. 338), Syriac bishop and teacher, according to tradition tried many times to climb Mount Ararat to find Noah's Ark, believed to be buried under thick layers of ice at Parrot Glacier on the top of the mountain. Resting close to the summit, in his sleep, an angel placed a fragment of the Ark close to him, and instructed him in a dream to awake. A spring with miraculous healing qualities bubbled up in the place where St. James had laid down. Later, a church bearing the saint's name was built nearby the stream. Until an earthquake in 1840 wiped it away, an Armenian monastery dedicated to St. Jacob of Nisibis stood on the northeastern slope of Mt. Ararat near the village of Akori, (close to the modern border between Armenian and Turkey).[19] Today Jacob's small, rectangular piece of wood is enshrined in the treasury of Holy Etchmiadzin in Armenia. This prayer is attributed to Jacob:

> Grant me from your mercy,
> so that through your mercy I may comprehend your love of humanity.
> Grant me grace to preach about you,
> so that all who listen may turn away in penance from their evil deeds.
> Touch me through love from your beneficence to proclaim your glory to humanity,
> so that those who listen may entreat you to forgive trespasses.
> Send to me the protector, your Holy Spirit,

---

17. Shnorhali, *Jesus, the Son*, 12.
18. Shnorhali, *Jesus, the Son*, 13.
19. Account in stjamesevanston.org. What is better documented is that Jacob was spiritual father to Ephrem, defended orthodoxy at the Council of Nicaea in 325 and was present at the dedication of the Church of the Holy Sepulcher, Jerusalem in 335.

so that through It I may be strengthened to speak about your invincible force . . .
By your finger you granted illumination to the great Moses to proclaim your divinity,
so also now illuminate me by the dawning of your light,
so that by your light I may illuminate the sons of your church.[20]

Searches for Noah's Ark have continued up to the present day.[21] But the important thing is to seek out its meaning and significance in times of uncertainty.

QUESTIONS FOR TODAY

Vocation of the Church

After a thousand years, we hear again the voices of Gregory and Nerses speaking into our situation. Nerses and Gregory remind us that it is best to approach the story of the Flood by appreciating its symbolic value: it can be read as parable or as allegory with much to teach us about the calling of the Christian community. It is an archetype, as we know found in many other cultures.[22] Its power remains as a metaphor enabling us to explore heuristically current events.

The image of the Flood is scarily apposite for the surge of the Covid 19 pandemic and its aftermath. We live in times of turbulence: the virus, increasing like rising floodwaters, threatens to engulf us and swamp our health systems. We may feel like vulnerable boats buffeted by storms and the weather forecast, as it were, is unpredictable and uncertain. We are all at sea, adrift. We're on the high seas of change with no land in sight. We crave an Ararat, safe harbor and fixed points by which to navigate our future. A sister working in the intensive care unit at the Royal London Hospital, referring to the unit being inundated by critically-ill patients puts it: "I've felt broken on many occasions. How I feel about this time: it's like I'm trapped in a cave and the water is slowly rising. I am barely keeping my head above water."[23]

---

20. Hilkins, "An Armenian Invocational Prayer," 270–271. Not all scholars accept this attribution.

21. National Geographic News April 30, 2010.

22. Epic of Gilgamesh is the best-known example, dated to 1800BC .

23. Sister Carleen Kelly interviewed in a report for BBC News, Myrie, "Royal London Hospital Reports."

What is the role of the church in such a time?

Gregory affirms: "The Church drives away pain, heals the infirm, overcomes the tyranny of demons... For sinners tossing about on the sea, she is a safe harbor."[24] Nerses calls the ark of the church "a shelter."

The church needs to re-imagine its role as an "ark of salvation" with courageous innovation faithful to its tradition. Since the twelfth century, churches in England have been places where vulnerable and threatened people can claim sanctuary and protection, and this idea has spread worldwide. Today church buildings discover a role as centers for community food banks and as centers for mass vaccination. As I write, historic Salisbury and Litchfield cathedrals in the UK, for many centuries places of pilgrimage and healing, have been transformed into health centers. Their nave—the Latin the word "navis" means ship—are filled with stations administering life-saving jabs.

Buildings can provide shelter but sanctuary is best provided in human community and relationships. We are experimenting with other expressions of community, welcome and hospitality. We have the biblical mandates. Noah's Ark welcomed creatures "of every kind"—"clean and unclean" (Gen 7:8)—an image of inclusivity and non-judgmental acceptance. The Hebrew prophets consistently help "the widow, the stranger and the orphan" (Exod 22:21,22; Deut 10:18; 14:29). Jesus affirmed this priority in his Nazareth manifesto:

> The Spirit of the Lord is upon me,
>   because he has anointed me
>   to bring good news to the poor.
> He has sent me to proclaim release to the captives
>   and recovery of sight to the blind,
>   to let the oppressed go free... (Luke 4:18)

Today these groups of people are represented by older people in care, children in danger, and asylum seekers—those who feel isolated and cut off from others. We need to ask: who are the people who are lacking financial, communal, emotional, and other support networks? Who is hurting the most, and has the least resources of support? By telephone calls and social media, by writing letters and making doorstep visits to neighbors, by building online virtual sanctuaries, safe spaces where people are honored and not judged, we begin to model self-sacrifice and connect with people, listen, and support. In times of social distancing we can overcome isolation

---

24. Gregory of Narek, *Speaking with God*, Prayer 75l, 251–52.

with gestures of love that affirm and hearten, a love that knows no bounds. Recently Pope Francis has written: "The good news is that an Ark awaits us to carry us to a new tomorrow. Covid-19 is our Noah moment, as long as we can find our way to the Ark of the ties that unite us: of love, and of a common belonging."[25] We are being summoned from individualism towards human solidarity, from egocentrism to building community, from atomization towards a sense that we belong to each other, from personal ambition to working for the common good—as we find ourselves together on a shared journey into a new future.

Conceptions of God

The voices from Mount Ararat call us to re-evaluate and revisit our ideas of God. Both Nerses and Gregory discover a God of new beginnings—both in the story of the Flood and the renewal of the world, and in their own experience of finding healing. The world begins anew after the calamity and a dove with an olive sprig becomes a symbol of hope (Gen 8:11). The peak of Ararat, emerging from the waters, is a sign of hope, the pledge of a fresh start. God promises a new dawn for creation:

> As long as the earth endures,
> > seedtime and harvest, cold and heat,
> summer and winter, day and night,
> > shall not cease (8:22).

> Be fruitful and multiply, abound on the earth (9:7).

> This is the sign of the covenant that I make between me and you
> and every living creature that is with you, for all future generations:
> I have set my bow in the clouds,
> it shall be a sign of the covenant between me and the earth (9:12,13).

Reflecting on this, Peter in some way sees the story of the Flood pre-figuring the paschal mystery:

> God waited patiently in the days of Noah, during the building of the ark, in which a few, that is, eight persons, were saved through water. And baptism, which this prefigured, now saves you—not as a removal of dirt from the body, but as an appeal to God for a good conscience—through the resurrection of Jesus Christ, who

---

25. Pope Francis, *Let us Dream*, 15.

has gone into heaven and is at the right hand of God, with angels, authorities, and powers made subject to him. (1 Peter 3:20–22)

Such a dying and rising God refreshes us compassionately, equips bold responses to trial, and sustains hope in time of calamity.

FOR PERSONAL REFLECTION

1. What words from Ararat resonate with your present experience?
2. In time of crisis do you batten down the hatches in defensive self-protective mode or dare, like Nerses, to open a window to the dove of the Holy Spirit?
3. How can the church be a place of refuge and ark of salvation in our own turbulent and uncertain times?
4. In what ways might your experience of stormy waters lead you closer to God?
5. If your soul were a ship or vessel what kind would it be? (Confident ocean-going liner, refugee's vulnerable dinghy, tanker, fishing boat, Celtic coracle, ark . . . ?) What is this image telling you?
6. What kind of God are you discovering at this time?

Photo courtesy sacredsites.com

2

Sinai

Encountering the Divine in Darkness and in Light

> *The Lord is king! Let the earth rejoice;*
>   *let the many coastlands be glad!*
> *Clouds and thick darkness are all around him;*
>   *righteousness and justice are the foundation of his throne.*
> *Fire goes before him,*
>   *and consumes his adversaries on every side.*
> *His lightnings light up the world;*
>   *the earth sees and trembles.*
> *The mountains melt like wax before the Lord,*
>   *before the Lord of all the earth.*
>   *Light dawns for the righteous,*
>   *and joy for the upright in heart. (Ps 97: 1–5, 11)*

THROUGHOUT HISTORY, THE SINAI peninsula has been a crucial crossroad because of its strategic position linking east with west, and north with south, witnessing the crossing in the Exodus of the Israelites from Egypt to Canaan. Bounded by the Mediterranean to the north, the Red Sea to the west, and the Gulf of Aqaba to the east, the Sinai peninsula forms a bridge between Asia and Africa. The red granite rock of the Sinai massif, also known as Jebel Mousa (Mount Moses) or Mount Horeb soars to 2285 meters above the wide plain in glorious isolation, its stratified layers of rock a palette of rusts and browns.

The biblical narrative tells us that the Israelites trembled when they first saw it. It is a place of paradox, intimidating yet strangely inviting. It terrified the Israelites who must not touch it on pain of death, yet it welcomed the elderly figure of Moses. It looks bleak and inhospitable yet it conceals, amidst its rugged peaks, little plateaux of fertility, where the first hermits planted orchards and lived in caves. They came to the holy mountain in the third century and established at the foot of the mountain at the site of the Burning Bush the main monastery, which Justinian in the sixth century consolidated and fortified as a kind of desert fortress. The first monastics came to the Sinai in their yearning to draw near to God in the midst of profound silence and isolation. It is estimated that by the seventh century there were some six hundred monastics living in the region of Sinai. We will be meeting Sinaite monks John Climacus, Philotheos and Hesychios, and also hearing the voice of Gregory of Nyssa.

Today the summit can be reached from the monastery by two different routes. The 3,750 Steps of Repentance ascending to the very summit were constructed in the sixth century. In the nineteenth century, Abbas Pasha I created the alternate Camel Trail, a more circuitous and more gradual ascent, that coincides with the Steps of Repentance for the last ascent of 750 steps. Near the apex a cave is actually a cleft in the rock, considered to be the place where Moses was hidden by God and from where he beheld the glory of God: "while my glory passes by I will put you in a cleft of the rock, and I will cover you with my hand until I have passed by" (Exod 33:22). From the crest one has astonishing views of the Sinai Peninsula by day, while at night the sky is so clear and unpolluted by light that one can see galaxies: faraway stars and constellations glinting like diamonds in the midst of inky blackness, a sheen of strange light clothing the dark mountains of earth.

EGERIA (c350-c415), the intrepid the Spanish pilgrim described in the remarkable diary of her travels her encounter with the mountain as she approached across the plain in 348:

> [The Mount of God] looks like a single mountain as you are going round it, but when you actually go into it there are really several peaks, all of them known as "the Mount of God", and the principal one, the summit on which the Bible tells us that "God's Glory came down", is in the middle of them. I never thought I had seen

mountains as high as those which stood around it, but the one in the middle where God's glory came down was the highest of all, so much so that, when we were on top, all the other peaks we had seen and thought so high looked like little hillocks far below us. Another remarkable thing—it must have been planned by God—is that even though the central mountain, Sinai proper on which God's glory came down, is higher than all the others, you cannot see it until you arrive at the very foot of it to begin your ascent. After you have seen everything and come down, it can be seen facing you, but this cannot be done till you start your climb. I realized it was like this before we reached the Mount of God, since the brothers had already told me, and when we arrived there I saw very well what they meant.[1]

Darkness or Light? Divine Disclosure or Concealment?

The Book of Exodus gives us an awesome and mysterious narrative:

> On the morning of the third day there was thunder and lightning, as well as a thick cloud on the mountain, and a blast of a trumpet so loud that all the people who were in the camp trembled. Moses brought the people out of the camp to meet God. They took their stand at the foot of the mountain. Now Mount Sinai was wrapped in smoke, because the LORD had descended upon it in fire; the smoke went up like the smoke of a kiln, while the whole mountain shook violently. As the blast of the trumpet grew louder and louder, Moses would speak and God would answer him in thunder. When the LORD descended upon Mount Sinai, to the top of the mountain, the LORD summoned Moses to the top of the mountain, and Moses went up (Exod 19:16–20)

> When all the people witnessed the thunder and lightning, the sound of the trumpet, and the mountain smoking, they were afraid and trembled and stood at a distance, and said to Moses, "You speak to us, and we will listen; but do not let God speak to us, or we will die." Moses said to the people, "Do not be afraid; for God has come only to test you and to put the fear of him upon you so that you do not sin." Then the people stood at a distance, while Moses drew near to the thick darkness where God was. (Exod 20: 18–21)

---

1. Wilkinson, *Egeria's Travels*, 55.

Sinai

> Then Moses went up on the mountain, and the cloud covered the mountain. The glory of the LORD settled on Mount Sinai, and the cloud covered it for six days; on the seventh day he called to Moses out of the cloud. Now the appearance of the glory of the LORD was like a devouring fire on the top of the mountain in the sight of the people of Israel. Moses entered the cloud, and went up on the mountain. Moses was on the mountain for forty days and forty nights. (Exod 24.15–18)

The awesome theophany on Mount Sinai is paradoxical. There is dazzling light, fire and lightening; there is dense shrouding darkness and impenetrable cloud. These can symbolize for us two approaches to God. We find God in light as he illumines our lives and makes us radiant with a sense of his presence. But we also encounter God in deep darkness—we cannot make anything out—we encounter the unknowable mystery of God, who is beyond the categories and concepts of human language. In Christian spirituality both approaches have their place: the cataphatic tradition, the *via positiva*, delighting in vivid metaphors and images, faces the *via negativa*, going beyond images, the way called apophatic—which means literally "the end of words." Spiritual writers strongly linked with Mount Sinai take opposite but complementary views, as we shall see.

Moses Himself Reveals the Paradox

Moses face shone radiantly because he had encountered God in the shining brightness of his glory. He also met with God in the deep darkness. Moses' dilemma reflects the two approaches we have seen. What will Moses do? Will he come down from the mountain, among his people, with unveiled face to show the Israelites that he had seen God's glory and indeed experienced divine illumination? Or would he veil his face to conceal the glory so that the Israelites would know nothing of the mystery of the encounter? Would Moses reveal or conceal? Would there be disclosure or hiddenness? This is what we wonder when we ascend the mount of prayer. Will we find God in startling discoveries, insights, revelations? Or will we experience mystery, clouds of unknowing, that we cannot articulate to others, a God beyond human words? Maybe we will like Moses choose both ways—keeping our veil on and remaining silent about our unspeakable encounter with God, or removing the veil so that we can share, somehow, the truths we have discovered about God. Paul for his part, was also ambivalent. He tells us to have unveiled faces: "all of us, with unveiled faces, seeing the glory of the Lord as though reflected in a mirror, are being transformed into the same image from one degree of glory to another; for this comes from the Lord, the Spirit" (2 Cor 3: 18). But in other places he will be more circumspect: "O the depth of the riches and wisdom and knowledge of God! How unsearchable are his judgments and how inscrutable his ways!" (Rom 11:33).

GREGORY OF NYSSA (335–95) in his *Life of Moses* reflects on the Christian vocation as a pilgrimage and journey for which the Israelites' escape from Pharaoh, their passage through the Red Sea, and their encounter with God at Sinai suggest a pattern or archetype that can be reflected in our own experience. The spiritual journey begins with baptism, prefigured in the crossing of the Red Sea, liberating a person from the captivity not of Pharaoh but of sin. The Christian pilgrim's journey, like the trek through the wilderness, will be marked by God's provision (as in manna, water from the rock), God's guidance (the pillar of cloud), human failure and spiritual battles (as represented in the conflict with Amalekites). Ultimately all this leads to the ascent of the mountain of divine knowledge, represented in Sinai. Gregory claims that an integral element in the Christian pilgrimage is the encounter with divine darkness, as it was for Moses:

> What does it mean that Moses entered the darkness and then saw God in it? What is now recounted seems to be contradictory to the first theophany [the Burning Bush], for then the Divine was beheld in light but now he is seen in darkness. Let us not think that this is at variance with the sequence of things we have contemplated spiritually. Scripture teaches by this that religious knowledge comes at first to those who receive it as light. Therefore what is perceived to be contrary to religion is darkness, and the escape from darkness comes about when one participates in light. But as the mind progresses and, through an ever greater and more perfect diligence, comes to perceive reality, as it approaches more nearly to contemplation, it sees more clearly what of the divine nature is uncontemplated.

It is a sign, then, of spiritual maturity and evidence that one is making progress in the spiritual life if one comes to encounter God in the darkness. Gregory goes on:

Sinai

> For leaving behind everything that is observed, not only what sense comprehends but also what the intelligence thinks it sees, it keeps on penetrating deeper until by the intelligence's yearning for understanding it gains access to the invisible and the incomprehensible, and there it sees God. This is the true knowledge of what is sought; this is the seeing that consists in not seeing, because that which is sought transcends all knowledge, being separated on all sides by incomprehensibility as by a kind of darkness. Wherefore John the sublime, who penetrated into the luminous darkness, says "No one has ever seen God", thus asserting that knowledge of the divine essence is unattainable not only by men but also by every intelligent creature.
>
> When, therefore, Moses grew in knowledge, he declared that he had seen God in the darkness, that is, that he had then come to know that what is divine is beyond all knowledge and comprehension, for the text says, "Moses approached the dark cloud where God was." What God? He who "made darkness his hiding place," as David says, who also was initiated into the mysteries in the same inner sanctuary.[2]

Gregory of Nyssa was the first writer to develop this message through the image of darkness; it was to become an important strand in thinking of spiritual development throughout the history of Christian spirituality. Danielou puts it: "In Gregory of Nyssa . . . the term 'darkness' takes on a new meaning and an essentially mystical connotation . . . Gregory's originality consists in the fact that he was the first to express this characteristic of the highest stages of mystical experience."[3] In Moses' first encounter with God, in the Burning Bush, God appears as light, as illumination. For Gregory, this represents the beginning of the Christian conversion, a turning from the darkness of falsehood to the light of Christ. This process of illumination, for beginners, involves a purification of the soul from foreign elements. However, as the Christian, like Moses, progresses along the spiritual journey, he or she is led into darkness: not a negative darkness but a "luminous darkness." This represents the unknowability of God: this is the apophatic spiritual path, which falls silent before the unspeakable mystery of God. Danielou puts it:

> After learning all that can be known of God, the soul discovers the limits of this knowledge; and this discovery is an advance, because

---

2. Gregory of Nyssa, *Life of Moses* 95.
3. Jean Danielou, "Introduction" in Musurillo, *From Glory to Glory*, 27.

now there is an awareness of the divine transcendence and incomprehensibility. We have then arrived at a negative, "apophatic" theology. For we have now an authentic experience, a true vision. And the darkness is a positive reality that helps us to know God—that is why it is called luminous. For it implies an awareness of God that transcends all determination, and thus it is far truer than any determined categorical knowledge. For here in this obscurity the soul experiences the transcendence of the divine nature, that infinite distance by which God surpasses all creation.[4]

For Gregory, the encounter with God in the dark is not a rarefied experience or only limited to Moses. He writes of his own brother Basil—whom we will meet later:

> Often we saw him enter the darkness where God was. By the mystical guidance of the Spirit he understood what was invisible to others, so that he seemed to be enveloped in that darkness in which the Word of God is concealed.[5]

Andrew Louth explains: "It is an experience beyond the senses and beyond the intellect; it is a feeling awareness of a fragrance that delights and enraptures the soul."[6]

In the fifth century, the writer known as Dionysius develops in his *Mystical Theology* the thought of Gregory:

> Trinity!! Higher than any being,
>   any divinity, any goodness!
> Guide of Christians
>   in the wisdom of heaven!
> Lead us up beyond unknowing and light,
>   up to the farthest, highest peak
>   of mystic scripture,
>   where the mysteries of God's Word
>   lie simple, absolute and unchangeable
>   in the brilliant darkness of a hidden silence.
> Amid the deepest shadow
>   they pour overwhelming light
>   on what is most manifest.

---

4. Jean Danielou, "Introduction" in Musurillo, *From Glory*, 30. Gregory also develops this in his interpretation of the Song of Songs where the divine darkness is characterized not only by unknowing but also by desire and yearning on the part of the bride.

5. "To His Brother Basil" in Migne, *Patrologia Graeca* 46, 812.

6. Louth, *Origins*, 93.

Sinai

> Amid the wholly unsensed and unseen
> they completely fill our sightless minds
> with treasures beyond all beauty.[7]

Dionysius echoes the thought of Gregory of Nyssa; indeed, he seems to have known his *Life of Moses*—he too uses a similar image to explore the significance of darkness. Thus he writes:

> Leave behind you everything perceived and understood, everything perceptible and understandable, all that is not and all that is, and, with your understanding laid aside, strive upward as much as you can toward union with him who is beyond all being and knowledge. By an undivided and absolute abandonment of yourself and everything, shedding all and freed from all, you will be uplifted to the ray of the divine shadow which is above everything that is.[8]

Within his Christianized Neo-Platonism, Dionysius finds the apex of the spiritual search.[9]

JOHN CLIMACUS (579–649), revered by the Eastern Churches, is little heard in the West. We do not know much about him—references in his writings to the sea suggest he may have grown up in the seventh century in a place like Gaza. Here monastic life was flourishing and discovery of its opportunities led John to search for a deeper encounter with God, a quest leading him to Mount Sinai where he joined the Vatos Monastery at the foot of the holy mountain (pre-cursor to St Catherine's). At sixty-five years of age, he became Abbot. Pondering the challenge and invitation of Mount Sinai, John composed his masterpiece *The Ladder of Divine Ascent*. He employs the analogy of Jacob's Ladder as the framework for his spiritual teaching, and each chapter is a "step". There are thirty steps of the ladder: the first seven concern general virtues necessary for the ascetic life, while the next nineteen (steps 8–26) give instruction on overcoming vices and building their corresponding virtues. The final four steps concern the higher virtues toward which the ascetic life aims. The final rung of the ladder—beyond prayer, stillness, and even dispassion—is love. Originally written for monks of a neighboring monastery, the *Ladder* swiftly became a much-beloved

---

7. Pseudo-Dionysius, *Complete Works*, 135. See Louth, *Denys the Aeropagite*.
8. Pseudo-Dionysius, *Complete Works*, 135.
9. See perspective in McGinn, *Foundation of Mysticism*.

book of Byzantine spirituality, widely read by Orthodox Christians in the season of Lent.

John tells us that we need on our spiritual journey a companion, a soul-friend or spiritual director, akin to Moses:

> Those of us who wish to get away from Egypt, to escape from Pharaoh, need some Moses to be our intermediary with God, to stand between action and contemplation, and stretch out his arms to God, that those led by him may cross the sea of sin and put to flight the Amalek of the passions. Those who have given themselves up to God but imagine that they can go forward without a leader are surely deceiving themselves. The fugitives from Egypt had Moses . . . like those who heal the passions of the soul by the care of doctors; they are the ones who have come out of Egypt.[10]

John asks us to reflect on the progress we are making in our ascent to God:

> I have put together a ladder of ascent, though my meager knowledge makes me something of a second-rate architect. Still, let each one take note of the step on which he is standing. Is it on the step of self will, of fame, of a loose tongue, of hot temper? Or of possessiveness? Is it on the step of atonement for sin, of greater zeal, of loving fire added to fire?[11]

For John love is the summit and goal of the journey:

> Most beautiful of all the virtues . . . enlighten us, end our thirst, lead us, show us the way, since we long to soar up to you. You rule everything, and now you have enraptured my soul. I am unable to hold in your flame, and therefore I will go forward praising you . . .[12]

With Mount Sinai towering above his monastery, John has questions for us:

> That climb, how was it? Tell me, for I long to know. What is the mode, what is the law joining together those steps that the lover has set as an ascent in his heart? (cf. Ps 83:6). I thirst to know the number of those steps, and the time required to climb them . . .

---

10. Climacus (trans. Luibheid and Norman Russell), *Ladder,* 74. The reference is to Exod 17:11–13 where in the battle against the Amalekites (representing the passions) the intercessory arms of Moses are held up by both Hur (action) and Aaron (contemplation).

11. Climacus (trans. Luibheid and Norman Russell), *Ladder* 265.

12. Climacus (trans. Luibheid and Norman Russell), *Ladder,* 289.

> Ascend, my brothers, ascend eagerly. Let your hearts' resolve be to climb. Listen to the voice of the one who says: "Come let us go up to the mountain of the Lord, to the house of our God" (Isa 2:3). [13]

John also wrote a shorter work *To the Shepherd* (Latin: *Liber ad Pastorem*). To encourage one in the practice of being a pastor and spiritual leader, Climacus says: "Let the great Moses be a model for you."[14] In contrast to Gregory of Nyssa, John delights in the primary experience of divine light:

> His footsteps you follow, O most patient man . . . and ever proceeding to a new height, you have even a little surpassed him . . . the mountain you have ascended, and have beheld God by means of a thorny and rugged manner of life, and received the divine voice and illumination. You have loosed the sandal, that is, this entire mortal sheath . . . wherefore the Lord has entrusted you, as to one unshakeable, the leadership of the brethren, whom, O guide of guides, you have separated and fearlessly freed from Pharaoh and the polluted brick-making of the clay, and through your great experience have transmitted to them the divine fire and the cloud of purity which extinguishes every flame of desire.
>
> You have ascended to the heights, you have dispelled all manner of darkness and gloom and tempest—I mean the thrice gloomy darkness of ignorance. You have drawn nigh to that light which is far more awesome, brilliant and sublime than the flame in the bush . . . You have been deemed worthy of the voice, of divine vision and of prophecy. You saw, perhaps, while still in this life, future things from behind (Exod 33:23)—I mean that illumination of knowledge which will come to pass in the last times. Thereupon, by means of this voice, you heard "a man shall not see" (Exod 33:20) and from the vision of God in Horeb you descended into that deep vale of humility, furnished with the tablets of mystic ascent, and with the countenance of both your soul and your body glorified . . . you have drawn high to the holy mountain, and fixing your eye upon Heaven, you have set your foot upon its base, and run, and gone up . . . you have gone before us on the road and led the way.[15]

Like Moses it can be said of the pastor: "You have transmitted to them the divine fire."[16]

---

13. Climacus (trans. Luibheid and Norman Russell), *Ladder*, 289, 291.
14. Climacus (trans. Moore), *Ladder*, 246.
15. Climacus (trans. Moore), *Ladder*, 247.
16. Climacus (trans. Moore), *Ladder*, 247.

Voices from the Mountains

HESYCHIOS THE PRIEST was Abbot of the Monastery of the Mother of God of the Burning Bush at Mount Sinai, probably in the later seventh century.[17] He owes a debt to St John Climacus and with Philotheos, whom we shall meet shortly, the three of them make up a sort of Sinai School with their common teaching on watchfulness, inner attentiveness and the guarding of the heart.

> Watchfulness is a spiritual method which, if sedulously practised over a long period, completely frees us with God's help from impassioned thoughts, impassioned words and evil actions. It leads, insofar as this is possible, to a sure knowledge of the inapprehensible God, and helps us to penetrate the divine and hidden mysteries. It enables us to fulfil every divine commandment in the Old and New Testaments and bestows on us every blessing of the age to come.[18]
>
> The great lawgiver Moses—or rather the Holy Spirit—indicates the pure, comprehensive and ennobling character of this virtue, and teaches us how to acquire and perfect it, when he says: "Be attentive to yourself, lest there arise in your heart a secret thing which is an iniquity" (Deut 15:9 LXX) . . . Watchfulness is a way of embracing every virtue, every commandment. It is the heart's stillness and, when free from mental images, it is the guarding of the intellect.[19]

The intellect is a key concept in Hesychios and other writers: it denotes not clever or academic thought, as we might read it, but rather a receptive and longing heart.[20]

Pondering Moses' extraordinary life-journey and his encounter with God on Sinai, Hesychios views Moses as a kind of archetype or model:

> The Fathers regard Moses the Lawgiver as an ikon of the intellect [the receptive heart]. He saw God in the burning bush (Exod 3), his face shone with glory . . . he led Israel out of bondage. These

---

17. He is to be distinguished from fifth century Hesychius of Jerusalem who we will meet in chapter 7.

18. Hesychios in Palmer et al, *Philokalia Vol.1*, 162.

19. Hesychios in Palmer et al, *Philokalia Vol.1*, 162.

20. Defined as "The highest facility in humanity, through which—provided it is purified—one knows God . . . by means of direct apprehension or spiritual perception . . . The intellect does not function by formulating abstract concepts and then arguing on this basis to a conclusion reached through deductive reasoning, but it understands divine truth by means of immediate experience, intuition . . . the intellect dwells in the depths of the soul; it constitutes the innermost aspect of the heart." Palmer et al, *Philokalia Vol.1*, 262.

Sinai

happenings, when seen metaphorically and spiritually are activities and privileges of the intellect [receptive heart].[21]

Hesychios teaches that there are various types of watchfulness, requiring an acute alertness to the intrusion into our consciousness of negative or distracting thoughts. He urges us to deal decisively with them so that we can attain a purity of heart and maintain an openness to God:

> One type of watchfulness consists in carefully scrutinizing every mental image of provocation . . .
> A second type of watchfulness consists in freeing the heart from all thoughts, keeping it profoundly silent and still, and in praying.
> A third type consists in continually and humbly calling upon the Lord Jesus Christ for help.[22]
> A further type [is] also effective: this is to fix one's gaze on heaven and to pay no attention to anything material.[23]

Hesychios notices a progression in the receptivity of heart and mind, and shows how he stands in the cataphatic tradition of spirituality, open to divine illumination:

> While we are being strengthened in Christ Jesus and beginning to move forward in steadfast watchfulness, He at first appears in our intellect like a torch which, carried in the hand of the intellect, guides us along the tracks of the mind; then He appears like a full moon, circling the heart's firmament; then He appears to us like the sun, radiating justice, clearly revealing Himself in the full light of spiritual vision.[24]

Hesychios uses language echoing the theophany to Moses on Mount Sinai, suggesting that we may become a sort of Sinai, place of divine revelation, in ourselves:

> The guarding of the intellect may appropriately be called "light-producing", "lightening-producing", "light-giving" and "fire-bearing" for truly it surpasses endless virtues . . . Those who are seized by love for this virtue . . . are able to contemplate mystically and to theologize; and when they have become contemplatives, they

---

21. Hesychios in Palmer et al, *Philokalia Vol.1*, 186.
22. A reference to the Jesus Prayer.
23. Hesychios in Palmer et al, *Philokalia Vol.1*, 164–65.
24. Hesychios in Palmer et al, *Philokalia Vol.1*, 191.

> bathe in a sea of pure and infinite light, touching it ineffably and living and dwelling in it.[25]

> Let us hold fast therefore to prayer and humility for together with watchfulness they act as a burning sword against the demons. If we do this, we shall daily and hourly be able to celebrate a secret festival of joy within our hearts.[26]
>
> Those who gaze upwards towards the Divine . . . because of the taste of the Divine and the ecstasy of desire make their longing ever more intense and insatiable as they ascend, they do not stop until they reach the Seraphim . . .[27]

PHILOTHEOS OF SINAI lived at the Monastery at the foot of Sinai in the seventh or eighth century. His *Forty Texts on Watchfulness* inspire us to new levels of awareness:

> It is very rare to find people whose intelligence is in a state of stillness. Indeed, such a state is only to be found in those who, through their whole manner of life strive to attract divine grace and blessing to themselves. If, then, we seek—by guarding our intellect and by inner watchfulness—to engage in the noetic work[28] that is the true philosophy in Christ, we must begin by exercising self-control with regard to our food, eating and drinking as little as possible. Watchfulness may fittingly be called a path leading both to the kingdom within us and to that which is to be; while noetic work that trains and purifies the intellect and changes it from an impassioned state to a state of dispassion, is like a window full of light through which God looks, revealing Himself to the intellect.[29]

He too teaches that a human person can become a Sinai—a "place of God" where God sets his presence, an inner mountain, as it were, where God may reveal himself:

> Where humility is combined with the remembrance of God that is established through watchfulness and attention, and also with recurrent prayer inflexible in its resistance to the enemy, there is

---

25. Hesychios in Palmer et al, *Philokalia Vol.1*, 192.
26. Hesychios in Palmer et al, *Philokalia Vol.1*, 193.
27. Hesychios in Palmer et al, *Philokalia Vol.1*, 198.
28. Noetic refers to the work of the intellect as understood above, and to intuitive perception of the Divine
29. Philotheos in Palmer et al, *Philokalia Vol.3*, 17.

Sinai

> the place of God, the heaven of the heart in which because of God's presence no demonic army dares to make a stand.[30]

> At every hour and moment let us guard the heart with all diligence from thoughts that obscure the soul's mirror; for in that mirror Jesus Christ, the wisdom and power of God the Father (1 Cor 1:24), is typified and luminously reflected. And let us unceasingly seek the kingdom of heaven inside our heart (Luke 17:21), the seed (Luke 13:19), the pearl (Matt 13:45) and the leaven (Matt 13:33). Indeed, if we cleanse the eye of the intellect we will find all things hidden within us. This is why our Lord Jesus Christ said that the kingdom of heaven is within us, indicating that the Divinity dwells in our hearts.[31]

Philotheos seems to hold together the cataphatic and apophatic, speaking of the heart as containing the uncontainable God:

> Let us go forward with the heart completely attentive and the soul fully conscious. For if attentiveness and prayer are daily joined together, they become like Elijah's fire-bearing chariot (2 Kgs 2:11), raising us to heaven. What do I mean? A spiritual heaven, with sun, moon, and stars, is formed in the blessed heart of one who has reached a state of watchfulness, or who strives to attain it; for such a heart, as a result of mystical contemplation and ascent, is enabled to contain within itself the uncontainable God. If then, you aspire to holiness, try with God's help to invoke the Lord and wholeheartedly to turn words into actions.[32]

> When invoked in prayer. Jesus draws near, He illumines the heart; for the remembrance of Him confers on us spiritual enlightenment and the highest of all blessings . . . Hence we must always breathe God . . .[33]

Our three voices from Sinai itself—John, Philotheos and Hesychios—develop similar themes that cluster around the crucial call to watchfulness—spiritual alertness to God and active vigilance over one's thoughts. As they pondered the experience of Moses on Sinai and sought to advance their own spiritual life they recognized that two key things are needed:

30. Philotheos in Palmer et al, *Philokalia Vol.3*, 17.
31. Philotheos in Palmer et al, *Philokalia Vol.3*, 25.
32. Philotheos in Palmer et al, *Philokalia Vol.3*, 26, 27.
33. Philotheos in Palmer et al, *Philokalia Vol.3* 27.

purity of heart—a sort of transparency and utter openness to God—safeguarded by an inner attentiveness. Both make possible a state of receptivity: an ability, as Moses displayed, to listen to and actually hear in some sense the divine voice, both in times of darkness and light.

QUESTIONS FOR TODAY

Through the pandemic we have tried stay positive by holding onto blessings and by celebrating the shafts of light that have shone upon us. We have discovered fresh ways of appreciating creation, especially since lockdowns reduced pollution and traffic noise, and we have rejoiced to hear birdsong once again in our cities. We have come to a renewed appreciation of others, and understood more deeply than ever before our human inter-connectedness and solidarity, and the fact that we really do need each other. We have realized that we must never take things for granted: all is gift, not right. We have had new opportunities to enjoy the gifts and graces of the Holy Spirit: we have seen new truths about compassion, self-sacrifice. We have witnessed courage and big-hearted responses to those in need. We increased our awareness of the poor and marginalized and have been re-sensitized to the isolated. Perhaps we have been learning how to convert unchosen loneliness into God-bearing solitude, isolation into spiritual retreat. We have exulted in the creativity shown by so many, not least the dedication and brilliance of scientists discovering new vaccines. Such learnings are to be celebrated as light, as illumination of soul, even as enlightenment—as we heard in the voices of John Climacus, Philotheos of Sinai and Hesychios the Priest. We may never be the same again!

But we have also found ourselves plunged into many kinds of darkness. Some of these darknesses have been experienced as very negative times, including the darkness of fear, the gloom of bereavement, the shadows of despair. We have lingered in the darkness of unresolved issues, unanswered questions, uncertainty and even agnosticism—not knowing—unknowing. We have been in a land of confusion and in a place of disorientation.

But maybe we can begin to see that God is in the darkness and in the questions. Gregory of Nyssa noted that Moses was in the thick darkness with God (Exod 20:21) and he re-assures us that it is actually OK to be in the dark, with God. God works in the dark. The darkness reminds us that God, sometimes revealing, is often infuriatingly, frustratingly incomprehensible, unknowable. It may feel as if he is present in times of light and absent in times of dark but actually he is waiting to be found in the dark. As Matthews cautions us, this summons us to a different mindset, and an expansion of our normal patterns of thought: "We have become used to thinking of the Christian faith in terms of the light that it provides, the illumination that it gives to the mind and soul. To understand it as a step into darkness requires a different frame of mind, a change of attitude for which we are little prepared."[34]

Yet this has been the challenge and opportunity of recent times. In hindsight, it may turn out to be life-transforming—the realization that in the dark we can watch and wait with God, that he is not faraway, he is close, even if unseen and unheard. On another mountain, Mount Nebo, looking back at the end of his life over his long journey through Sinai, Moses affirms the dawning of light on dark Sinai:

> This is the blessing with which Moses, the man of God, blessed the Israelites before his death. He said:
>
> The LORD came from Sinai,
>   and dawned from Seir upon us;
>   he shone forth from Mount Paran.
> With him were myriads of holy ones;
>   at his right, a host of his own.
> Indeed, O favorite among peoples,
>   all his holy ones were in your charge;
> they marched at your heels,
>   accepted direction from you.
> Moses charged us with the law,
>   as a possession for the assembly of Jacob . . .
>   Blessed by the LORD be his land,
>   with the choice gifts of heaven above,
>   and of the deep that lies beneath;
>   with the choice fruits of the sun,
>   and the rich yield of the months;
>   with the finest produce of the ancient mountains,
>   and the abundance of the everlasting hills;
>   with the choice gifts of the earth and its fullness,
>   and the favor of the one who dwells on Sinai.
> (Deut 33:1–4, 13–16)

---

34. Matthews, *Both Alike to Thee*.

FOR PERSONAL REFLECTION

1. John Climacus says: "let each one take note of the step on which he is standing." How would you describe where you are right now in your journey with God?

2. Have you experienced any "Burning Bush" times or Mount Sinai times of enlightenment and illumination? Recall these moments and celebrate them.

3. Danielou writes: "The darkness is a positive reality that helps us to know God." Reflect on times of darkness in your life that actually led you to new insight or a deeper appreciation of truth.

4. How do you feel when you find yourself as it were in darkness and thick cloud, faced with the unknowability and incomprehensibility of God?

5. How can we change bewilderment into wonderment?

3

Carmel
Forging Prophets and Mystics

> *You hold your head as high as Mount Carmel...*
> *How beautiful and charming you are, my love, with your elegance.*
> *(Song 7:5, 6, GW)*

MOUNT CARMEL RISES STEEPLY from the glittering waters of the Mediterranean, dominating the peninsula which protrudes from Israel's sweeping coastline at present day Haifa. It is stunningly forested with luxuriant vegetation of oak, pine, olive and laurel trees. Its eastern slope faces the broad Jezreel Valley with Mediggo to the north east and mysterious Tabor in the distance. This sheltered leeward side of the mountain is marked with fertile valleys and steep ravines, and among the springs is the Fountain of Elijah where the first Carmelites settled. Carmel is not a single peak but a range of mountains, sixteen miles long and two thousand feet high. Its name comes from the Hebrew *Karem El*, meaning the vineyards of God. Isaiah celebrated its beauty:

> The wilderness and the dry land shall be glad,
>   the desert shall rejoice and blossom;
>   like the crocus it shall blossom abundantly,
>   and rejoice with joy and singing.
>   The glory of Lebanon shall be given to it,

> the majesty of Carmel and Sharon.
> They shall see the glory of the LORD,
> > the majesty of our God. (Isa 35:1,2)

A present-day Carmelite echoes this thought:

> A desert carefully tended becomes a garden. In the imagination of the Carmelites, Mount Carmel represents not only the solitude in which the hermit wrestles demons, but it also represents the flowering of new, verdant life. The invitation to Carmel offered by the tradition is an invitation to open one's life to the loving activity of God and so to the blossoming of one's life. The garden is a counter-symbol to the desert. Mount Carmel represented solitude and stark battle to the Carmelite, but it was also a place of physical beauty which offered fresh water, thick forest, striking vistas, and the company of wild animals.[1]

An early Carmelite document, *The Institution of the First Monks*, waxes lyrical about Carmel's ideal conditions for prayer:

> The mountain does indeed afford silence and quiet to a hermit because of its solitude; shelter in its caves; peace in its woodlands; healthful air from its elevation; abundant food from its herbs and fruits; and delicious water from its springs.[2]

Elijah's Adventures

It is Elijah, of course, who first draws us to such an intoxicating mountain. Elijah is indeed one of the greatest heroes of the Old Testament, but his influence is not limited to his own time. In fact, he becomes an icon or archetype. Some four hundred years after Elijah's time, the prophet Malachi, in the last verses of the Old Testament, writes: "Behold, I will send you Elijah the prophet before the great and terrible day of the Lord comes. And he will turn the hearts of the fathers to their children . . ." (Mal 4:5,6). Elijah comes to represent the precursor of the messiah. In Jewish tradition a place is set for Elijah at every Passover meal, in expectation of his return to usher in the age of the Kingdom. In the New Testament, Elijah is remembered as "strong and mighty" (Luke 1:17, GNT), and is hailed as the greatest of all

---

1. Welch, *Carmelite Way*, 13.
2. "The Institution of the First Monks" (trans. Norman Werling) quoted in Welch, *Carmelite Way*, 54.

the prophets. Jesus remembers his courageous and powerful ministry (Luke 4:25), and Elijah appears besides Moses in the vision of the transfiguration (Matt 17:3). Jesus recognizes his ministry fulfilled in the person of John the Baptist (Matt 17:10–13). Paul recalls his prayer in the face of overwhelming odds (Rom 11:2–4), while James holds him up as an example of an intercessor whose prayer have "great power in its effect" (Jas 5:16b).

He lived in one of the darkest chapters of Israel's history. The reigning king Ahab was evil (see 1 Kgs 16.30) and easily manipulated by his wife Jezebel. The daughter of a priest of a Phoenician fertility cult, she was a cruel and domineering woman intent on promoting the religion of her Baal deities throughout the kingdom of Israel. Elijah steps onto the scene from obscure origins. What, precisely, was the task given him by God? He is to uphold standards of righteousness in the monarchy, and confront Ahab when he strays. But Elijah is ambitious for Yahweh and throws himself into a life of risk-taking. He encapsules the challenge for all of us to balance action and contemplation, stillness and movement. As we shall see, for Elijah this was a struggle—to achieve a resolution of the tension between the polarities of the call to proclaim a message and the call to listen to God in silence.

The Elijah cycle of stories opens with him speaking God's word of judgement to Ahab, and immediately placing himself in the firing line. God immediately says to him: "Go from here and turn eastward, and hide yourself by the Wadi Cherith, which is east of the Jordan. You shall drink from the wadi, and I have commanded the ravens to feed you there" (1 Kgs 17:3–4). Before he goes any further in his prophetic mission, God directs Elijah to a place of contemplation. It is vital that before he commits himself to a life of prophetic speaking and action, Elijah creates a space for silence, listening to God, and stillness. Like the Baptist and Jesus himself in the same desert, Elijah discovers that the prophetic vocation begins in silence.

Three years after the drought began, God asks him to return to Ahab and announce rain (18:2). When Elijah meets Ahab, he is hailed as "you troubler of Israel" (18:17), but Elijah responds that it is Ahab's idolatry which has brought trouble on the nation. Elijah is seized by an ambitious plan to show up the deficiency of Jezebel's gods. He challenges Ahab to a showdown, a face-to-face contest with the prophets of Baal. Ahab is to gather the people of Israel on Mount Carmel to witness this and make their choice.

Carmel

Facing Exhaustion

Elijah stands alone before the myriad ranks of Baal's prophets assembled on Mount Carmel. He asks them to set before their deity a sacrifice of a bull placed on wooden stakes, and challenges them to call down Baal to set it alight. They rant and rave for hours around their altar calling on Baal, meeting no answer. Then Elijah drenches his altar to the God of Israel with water to make the task of lighting the sacrifice even more difficult. He calls out in confidence to God, asking him to prove himself by sending fire from heaven. When God's fire falls, the people hail the true God of Israel, and Elijah leads the false prophets away to their doom.

Signs of rain appear on the horizon as Elijah looks out across the Mediterranean from his vantage point atop Carmel. The narrative continues: "Elijah went up to the top of Carmel; there he bowed himself down upon the earth and put his face between his knees" (1 Kgs 18:42). Signs that mental and physical exhaustion are already catching up with him emerge as Elijah climbs the summit of Carmel to get away from the crowd. But this momentous day is not over yet. Telling Ahab to return immediately to his base to avoid bad weather, Elijah insists on running ahead of Ahab's chariot—over a distance of some thirty miles! On arrival, Elijah is met by a messenger from Jezebel telling him she intends to murder him within twenty-four hours.

Greeted by these words, surely Elijah's heart begins to beat fast, pumping adrenaline again through his veins. He is now faced with a choice—in modern terms, "fight or flight?" Will he use his energy to struggle it out with his adversary, or will he retreat? He decides to flee for his life—going a considerable distance, over a hundred miles to Beersheba in the south of the country (19:1–3). There he ventures out into the Negev desert, alone. This represents a wilderness experience for Elijah, the desert symbolizing his inner state. As the winds blow across the empty plains, so a desolation sweeps over Elijah's soul. He comes to a place of brokenness. Elijah displays the classic indicators of "burnout", a form of breakdown. He is exhausted physically, and has been pushing his body far too far. He is drained spiritually, having burnt up all his inner resources in the contest on Carmel. He is depressed and succumbs to self-pity, turned in on himself. There is disillusionment and despair, as he realizes that his victory on Carmel has not ended Jezebel's plans to spread her idolatry throughout the country. It dawns on Elijah that his own goal for its instant extermination was unrealistic. He is overwhelmed by a sense of failure and powerlessness. There is a loss of self-confidence and self-esteem as he doubts his ability to continue his ministry. There is a crisis of vocation, as Elijah realizes that the task set him, the job he accepted from God, does not bring him fulfilment but frustration. Elijah has come to a point where he can talk with God, turning his heartaches into urgent prayer. His cry to God is honest and does not attempt to hide what he is feeling. The lines of communication are open—and this opens the way to a new future. This is catch-up time for him, as he comes to realize how crucial and indispensable is time alone with God, in the midst of active mission and ministry.

The Healing of Stress

How does God respond to his plight? In the silence Elijah discerns God's response, which is about recovery and pacing himself aright. There is a sense, in the account, of a clear set of priorities, an order and progression in God's plan of action for Elijah. First, God answers Elijah's physical needs of exhaustion: he gives him the gift of sleep (19:5). Then, through the agency of the angel, he gives him a hot meal and refreshing drink. Then more sleep is given. This is the first priority—to take efforts to restore the body.

Next, God invites Elijah to begin a journey, a pilgrimage (19:7) to Mount Sinai (Horeb), "the mount of God." In calling Elijah to Sinai, God is drawing him back to the wellsprings and fountain of his faith. It is time for Elijah to go back to basics, to return to the foundations and the essentials of faith. So, in the strength of food given him by God, Elijah treks further south to the very place where God first gathered together the people of Israel.

When Elijah arrives at Sinai, he retreats to a cave, and hiding in a dark corner, he waits there. God asks him, "What are you doing here, Elijah?" In these words, God is enquiring into his expectations. Is he really ready to meet God? Is he open to a renewal of his faith? Is he self-occupied, or will he be prepared to open himself to God? We can only receive from God when we are in a place of receptivity. We need to unburden ourselves totally of the negative thinking which has been clogging us up, so we can receive the re-energizing breath of God. Twice God gives Elijah an opportunity to empty himself of his doubts and fears—to get it decisively out of his system. Elijah pours forth his inner pain like a torrent before God. In this kind of prayer, we can expose our hidden fears to God, lower our barriers before him, and truthfully share our inner turmoil. If we first do this, then we can, like Elijah, begin to receive from God the graces he wants to give.

Carmel

God responds in three ways. First, he gives him a vision of himself; second, a practical plan of action, a set of priorities to guide his future; third, he corrects his false thinking. What is the meaning of the theophany Elijah is given? "And behold, the Lord passed by, and a great and strong wind rent the mountain, and broke in pieces the rocks before the Lord, but the Lord was not in the wind; and after the wind an earthquake, but the Lord was not in the earthquake; and after the earthquake a fire, but the Lord was not in the fire; and after the fire a still small voice" (19:12,13). Its clearest meaning, in the context of Elijah's life, is that God is not primarily interested in proving himself in great displays of power, in impressive demonstrations—as Elijah asked him to do on Carmel. The fire, the earthquake, the wind—all speak of stressful ways of working, noisy and disturbing—and God is not to be found in them. Rather he is to be discovered in the still small voice, in the silence. Elijah needs to change, indeed revolutionize his way of thinking. He must make time and space in his life so he will be able to listen and attend to God's voice speaking in the mind, the spirit, the conscience. This voice gets crowded out, drowned by incessant noise and activity. Elijah must learn the secret of stillness—to build into his ministry opportunities to be utterly silent before God, times when God is given a chance to minister to him, times when he can receive from God inner healing and a renewal of his spiritual resources. This is a vital safeguard against future burnout.

But God gives him another safeguard against the threat of stress. "And when Elijah heard it, he wrapped his face in his mantle, and went out and stood at the entrance of the cave" (19:13). Elijah is now leaving his place of hiding, coming out into the open, ready to see horizons again, ready to face the future. Mystic and activist Dorothy Soelle points out:

> [after] the experience of God in the "still, small voice" what happens now? Elijah does not withdraw into an act of worship; he does not make a pilgrimage to some shrine. Nor does he continue to divide things into the categories of sacred and profane, a division so dear to all religions. Instead, what happens is of significance for the Judeo-Christian tradition: the renewal of his political mission . . . he returns to the world.[3]

She is clear that prayer, if it involves a journey to a world within, must entail the remaking of the self—a re-energizing—so as to enable the return journey to the outer world without delay:

3. Soelle, *Inward Road*, 136.

> The goal is to reconcile the two worlds ... It seems almost impossible to reconcile the two: the magnitude of the inward journey which we need for experience of self, and the way back into the society of a world that can once more be lived in. Inwardness and involvement are not companion attributes in most people, for sensitive people are often not communally inclined, and people who like to be communally involved are sometimes lacking in sensitivity. Prayer and work, labor and contemplation appear to be compartmentalized into two worlds ... The critical question with respect to expression of the deepest human experiences, those we regard as "the inward journey", is the question of connection to and with society ... Living as Christ lived means the inward journey to the emptying and surrendering of the ego and the return journey to the midst of this world.[4]

We find in the journey within an encounter not only with God but a clarification of our own identity in God, our destiny, and our vocation in the world. Thus God gives Elijah a very specific action plan, a clear set of priorities. He cannot take on everything at once; he must see what is important and what is not. The tyranny of the present moment must pass; never again must Elijah allow himself to be overwhelmed by the enormity of his task. He must be realistic, he must plan, he must pace himself. God gives him three definite steps to take which will in fact transform the political landscape, anointing new kings for Syria and Israel. He does not need to worry right now about precisely how Ahab and Jezebel will be removed—that is in God's hands. He must be obedient to these imperatives, and everything else can wait. In the silence of the holy mountain, Elijah regains perspective and learns to listen to God.

We read about Elijah's subsequent career in 1 Kings 21 ~ 2 Kings 2. Is there a difference in him? Has he learned his lessons? He will again face potentially stressful situations, confronting Ahab over his ruthless exploitation of Naboth, and exposing his complicity in murder. But he keeps his composure and finds a ready, penitent response in his old adversary (21:27f). Elijah must also challenge Ahab's son about his error in consulting the foreign deities (2 Kgs 1). When he sends fifty soldiers to arrest him, they find Elijah "sitting on top of a hill" (2 Kgs 1:9). Has Elijah discovered at last a strategy for coping, a way of staying calm in the center of the storm? Has he finally applied the lesson of making time and space for solitude, for prayer, for God in the midst of a demanding prophetic lifestyle?

---

4. Soelle, *Inward Road*, 55, 56.

In the Steps of Elijah

Centuries later, seekers came to Mount Carmel, looking to the person of Elijah for inspiration. They were struck by his zeal and dedication. They admired his awareness of God's presence: "As the Lord of hosts lives, before whom I stand" (1 Kgs 18:15). In about AD 500, a monastery of Greek monks was formed and a church built on Mount Carmel. In the twelfth century Latin Christians came to Carmel, seeking to pattern themselves on the positive sides of Elijah's example. An early Carmelite narrative relates:

> We declare, bearing testimony to the truth, that from the time when the prophets Elijah and Elisha dwelt devoutly on Mount Carmel, holy Fathers both of the Old and the New Testament, whom the contemplation of heavenly things drew to the solitude of the same mountain, have without doubt led praiseworthy lives there by the fountain of Elijah in holy penitence unceasingly and successfully maintained.[5]

ALBERT OF JERUSALEM (c1150–215), living nearby at Acre, was asked to write in 1210 a Rule for these brothers to guide their developing lifestyle. He endeavored to strike a fine balance between action and stillness. The first monks interpreted Elijah's "double spirit" asked for by Elisha (2 Kgs 2:9) as representing the union of both the active and contemplative life, the "mixed life"—an integration of contemplative prayer and apostolic action. Though he was writing for the monks of Mount Carmel, Albert's guidelines can give us too valuable clues for ordering our life aright. His aim was to provide for the brothers of Carmel an integrated life, a life in which all time could be sanctified, "pondering the Lord's law day and night." Albert writes that "common sense is the guide of the virtues" and he proposes a carefully disciplined lifestyle that maintains a healthy equilibrium between four pairs of opposite commitments. Brundell observes: "Although the Rule of St Albert is clearly an attempt to be an alternative to the detailed structural models found at the time frequently in the way of life of the monks, yet it is above all else a document of spiritual guidance for those who wish to learn how to live a life 'meditating on the law of the Lord day and night.'"[6] Let us listen to his voice:

> Albert, called by God's favor to be Patriarch of the Church of Jerusalem, bids health in the Lord and the blessing of the Holy Spirit to

---

5. "Constitutions 1281" in Smelt, *Carmelites*, 40.
6. Michael Brundell, "Carmelite Spiritual Direction," 64.

his beloved sons in Christ, and the other hermits under obedience to him, who live near the spring on Mount Carmel.

Many and varied are the ways in which our saintly forefathers laid down how everyone, whatever his station or the kind of life he has chosen, should live a life of allegiance to Jesus Christ—how, pure in heart and steadfast in conscience, he must be unswerving in the service of his Master.

It is to me, however, that you have come for a rule of life in keeping with your avowed purpose, a rule you may hold fast to henceforward; and therefore:

If the Prior and brothers see fit, you may have foundations in solitary places, or where you are given a site that is suitable and convenient for the observance proper to your Order.

Next, each of you is to have a separate cell, situated as the land you propose to occupy may dictate, and allotted by disposition of the Prior with the agreement of the other brothers, or the more mature among them . . . .

However, you are to eat whatever may have been given you in a common refectory, listening together meanwhile to a reading from Holy Scripture where that can be done without difficulty.

Each one of you is to stay in his own cell or nearby, pondering the Lord's law day and night and keeping watch at his prayer unless attending to some other duty.

Those who know their letters and how to read the psalms should, for each of the hours, say those our holy forefathers laid down, and according to the Church's approved custom . . .

None of the brothers must lay claim to anything as his own, but your property is to be held in common; and each is to receive from the Prior—that is from the brother he appoints for the purpose—whatever befits his age and needs . . .

An oratory should be built as conveniently as possible among the cells, where, if it can be done without difficulty, you are to gather each morning to hear Mass.

On Sundays too, or other days if necessary, you should discuss matters of discipline and your spiritual welfare; and on this occasion the indiscretions and failings of the brothers, if any be found at fault, should be lovingly corrected.

You are to fast every day, except Sundays, from the feast of the Exaltation of the Holy Cross until Easter Day, unless bodily sickness or feebleness, or some other good reason, demand a dispensation from the fast; for necessity overrides every law.

Since man's life on earth is a time of trial, and all who live devotedly in Christ must undergo persecution, and the devil your foe is on the prowl like a roaring lion looking for prey to devour, you must use every care to clothe yourselves in God's armor so that you may be ready to withstand the enemy's ambush . . .

You must give yourselves to work of some kind, so that the devil may always find you busy; no idleness on your part must give him a chance to pierce the defenses of your souls . . . This is the way of holiness and goodness: see that you follow it.

The Apostle would have us keep silence, for in silence he tells us to work. As the Prophet also makes known to us: "Silence is the way to foster holiness." Elsewhere he says: "Your strength will lie in silence and hope." For this reason I lay down that you are to keep silence from Vespers until Morning Prayer the next day. At other times, although you need not keep silence so strictly, be careful not to indulge in a great deal of talk, for, as Scripture has it—and experience teaches us no less—"sin will not be wanting where there is much talk, and he who is careless in speech will come to harm"; and elsewhere: "The use of many words brings harm to the speaker's soul." And our Lord says in the Gospel: "Every rash word uttered will have to be accounted for on judgement day." Make a balance then, each of you, to weigh his words in; keep a tight rein on your mouths, lest you should stumble and fall in speech, and your fall be irreparable and prove mortal. Like the Prophet, watch your step lest your tongue give offense, and employ every care in keeping silent, which is the way to foster holiness . . .

Here then are the few points I have written down to provide you with a standard of conduct to live up to; but our Lord, at his second coming will reward anyone who does more than he is obliged to do. See that the bounds of common sense are not exceeded, however, for common sense is the guide of the virtues.[7]

Albert's Four Challenges

First, Albert insists on a balance between solitude and community, between being alone and interacting with others. He requires: "each of you is to have a separate cell", a space for living and praying which each monk could call his own. The Desert Fathers had taught "Go, sit in your cell, and your cell will teach you everything."[8] The cell becomes a symbol of the need to safe-

7. Edwards, "Rule of St Albert," 39–44.
8. Ward, *Sayings*, 139.

guard a space in our lives where we can be by ourselves, uninterrupted, and available to God in expectant, waiting, prayer.

Albert recognized the need to safeguard and protect from intrusion a place of privacy. There are times, he taught, that we must be entirely alone with God, as Elijah discovered, in order to listen attentively and without distraction to God. But there are also times when the community must come together, and he directs that the oratory or chapel must be "built as conveniently as possible among the cells." It represents the call to shared worship, the community at prayer. So too must the brothers eat in a common refectory, where they listen together to Scripture, and labor side-by-side at the communal tasks. The togetherness and aloneness must be held within a creative tension, the one sustaining the other.

Secondly, Albert proposes for the brothers on Mount Carmel a balance between work and prayer, activity and rest. He insists on the necessity of work for each of the brothers: "You must give yourselves to work of some kind, so that the devil may always find you busy; no idleness on your part must give him the chance to pierce the defenses of your souls." Albert says of the daily round of labor "this is the way of holiness and goodness; see that you follow it." But the day is to begin at the altar and be punctuated by periods of prayer. The Rule requires daily attendance at the Eucharist, and Carmelites see in the experience of Elijah nourished by bread from God on his pilgrimage to Sinai a sign of Communion sustaining us in daily life. In addition, there are seven times for common prayer each day—the canonical hours of the Daily Office, times for recollection using psalms of praise and petition. The whole day is to be marked by an alternating cycle of work and prayer.

Thirdly, Albert proposes for the brothers on Carmel a strict balance between silence and talking. Silence must be observed from Evening Prayer until morning. "At other times," he counsels, "although you need not keep silence so strictly, be careful not to indulge in a great deal of talk." Once again it is a question of proper perspective and Albert gives as his maxim: "make a balance, then, each of you." However, Albert is careful to make provision for the sharing of problems as they arise. The greatest day of worship should be a day too of honest reflection and exchange: "On Sundays, or other days if necessary, you should discuss matters of discipline and your spiritual welfare; and on this occasion the indiscretions and failings of the brothers, if any be found at fault, should be lovingly corrected." There is great wisdom in this direction to deal with problems as soon as they arise, not to procrastinate—avoiding the mistakes of Elijah.

Fourthly, Albert's Rule recommends a balance between sharing of resources and having what is needful: "None of the brothers must lay claim to anything as his own, but your property is to be held in common; and of such things as the Lord has given you each is to receive from the Prior— that is from the man he appoints for the purpose—whatever befits his age and needs." In this prescription he delivers the brothers from possessiveness and unnecessary attachments and encourages them to live in a spirit of simplicity, accepting gratefully what is needed for well-being.

Though these words were written for the first Carmelites, they point us towards a way to live without stress today. The Rule is not intended for slavish imitation, but is composed in a way that takes account of individual circumstances—for example, brothers are to fast during certain periods "unless bodily sickness or feebleness, or some other good reason, demand a dispensation from the fast; for necessity overrides every law." Albert understands human nature and makes allowances for weaknesses. His rule of thumb is: "See that the bounds of common sense are not exceeded." He is aware that this will be a struggle, and is emphatic: "you must use every care to clothe yourselves in God's armor so that you may be ready to withstand the enemy's ambush." Albert's Rule invites us to examine our lives and seek a sense of wholeness. Is there, for us, a balance between the needs of body, of mind, of spirit? If anything gets out of proportion—if there is work without prayer, or interaction with others without space for solitude—stress will result. It can be prevented, however, if we apply the principles Albert advocates for those first Carmelites, who tried to apply to themselves the lessons of Elijah's life.

The *Rule of St Albert* encouraged the spread of Carmelite communities throughout Europe. But over time, things began to get out of kilter. When Teresa of Avila (1515–1582) entered Carmelite life in sixteenth century Spain, she was horrified to discover how far Albert's original Rule had been distorted and corrupted. There were too many material comforts and an acquisitiveness had crept into the religious houses. But most of all she was dismayed by the imbalance between prayer and ministry. The sisters were forever leaving the enclosure to engage in charitable works and pastoral visiting, but there was little time for solitude left. Things had got out of balance. Teresa felt called to reform the Carmelite order and to invite her brothers and sisters to return to the basic disciplines of prayer and contemplation.

She recognized that without prayer, all our labors can be empty of meaning and of power; by prayer we are energized by God and can become channels and instruments of his grace.

A Hike in the Dark

JOHN OF THE CROSS (1542–91) wrote from a Spanish Carmelite tradition and he dreamt often of Mount Carmel, making it a symbol of the goal of prayer, union with God. The summit is depicted as an empty, expectant sacred space ready to be filled with the fullness of God. It is indeed an image of the spaciousness of soul that John sees as vital—an uncluttered openness to the Divine, a capacity to welcome the descending God, a receptivity to the transcendent one who longs to invade the soul if it is free of obstacles and blockages. John, a gentle and practical man who responded to hardship and rejection with big faith, holds before us an inspiring and realistic vision of the spiritual journey.

In the sketch of the mountain that accompanies his work *The Ascent of Mount Carmel* John pictures wide paths leading to dead ends and one narrow path leading directly to the crest. On this road John repeats several times the word *nada—nothing, nothing, nothing*. At the foot of the mountain John advises the climber:

> To reach satisfaction in all, desire satisfaction in nothing.
> To come to the knowledge of all, desire the knowledge of nothing.
> To come to possess all, desire the possession of nothing . . .
> In this nakedness the spirit finds its quietude and rest,
> for in coveting nothing, nothing tires it by pulling it up,
> and nothing oppresses it by pushing it down,
> because it is in the center of its humility.[9]

John is teaching that the secret of moving towards union with God is detachment, releasing our controlling grasp on things, letting go of worries, and giving up possessiveness. In order to make this climb we must relinquish unnecessary baggage and weights, and loosen our grip on anything that has become a distraction or preoccupation. In the spirit of Elijah, John is asking us to name our idols and dismiss them. He teaches that this does not require a monastic withdrawal from the world, but rather an attitude of having a lightness of touch towards it. He warns us about getting trapped

---

9. John of the Cross, *Collected Works*, 111.

in an unending cycle of materialism by "inordinate appetites", by which he means an addictive or manipulative attitude to things. There is "joy in temporal goods", he teaches, if we allow them to lead us to God and not away from him.

This may turn out to be a night-hike, for the pathway to the summit is tough, and John describes the experience in terms of the dark night of the soul that, in fact, turns out to be light-filled:

> O guiding night!
> O night more lovely than the dawn!
> O night that has united
> the Lover with his beloved,
> transforming the beloved in her Lover!

John explains why the path to the summit may be in darkness:

> We can offer three reasons for calling this journey toward union with God a night.
>
> The first has to do with the point of departure, because individuals must deprive themselves of their appetites for worldly possessions. This denial and privation are like a night for all one's senses.
>
> The second reason refers to the means or the road along which a person travels to this union. Now this road is faith, and for the intellect faith is also like a dark night.
>
> The third reason pertains to the point of arrival, namely God. And God is also a dark night to the soul in this life
>
> These three nights pass through a soul, or better, the soul passes through them in order to reach union with God.[10]

First, says John, in the dark we cannot actually see. In the deeper reaches of prayer, the Christian needs to shut down his or her five senses if they hold one captive in a state of attachment to the material world and activate one's self-seeking appetites.

Secondly, in the dark one cannot easily make out obstacles or turnings along the path, so one must move forward in trust. "We walk by faith, not by sight." In one's relationship with God, John teaches, one must take the risk of moving forwards without knowing the precise route, venturing into the unknown, where visibility is nil.

Thirdly, John says, the darkness speaks of God himself as Mystery. God is not something one can box in and neatly label—God is quite beyond

---

10. John of the Cross, *Collected Works*, 120.

humanity's best concepts and categories. But "the dark night of the soul" is not for John a negative experience, but rather a time of growth and healing. The night, for John, is a place of radical transformation. It represents a time when one allows God to do his work powerfully within, reshaping and redirecting the ego, and leading one into a greater surrender to him.

The darkness refers to a process of radical dispossession that John sees as lying at the heart of prayer. John sees prayer as a movement from egocentricity to God-centeredness, as a process in which God seeks to reshape us and convert the ego. What is needed is the renunciation of one's own confidences to enable a total surrender to God. The pain to be faced is the pain of letting go of being in control, the cost of being stripped of our egotistical powers. Follent puts it:

> The abandonment of self-mastery and the taking on of a radical dependence on God will necessarily be accompanied by a sense of being undone or being annihilated, yet such an anxiety is quite ungrounded. In fact, the discovery that one can no longer find one's guarantees in oneself may indeed be a sign that progress in the life with God is finally being achieved.[11]

The Mystical and the Prophetic

John himself was an active pastor and spiritual director and spoke prophetically to his Order in a critique of lax practice, seeking to bring back it to its radical roots—for which he was imprisoned in a dark cell for eight months. His biographers have estimated that after his ordination, he traveled nearly 18,000 miles all over Spain, mainly on foot. He reminds us, in the tradition of Elijah and Albert, that the challenge is to hold the contemplative and the prophetic together in a creative interplay in our lives. In his great poem *The Spiritual Canticle* John celebrates possibilities of encounters with the Divine that the mountain represents, but he does not imply we should to rest and luxuriate in intimate communion with Christ but rather let it fuel and empower our love as it issues in ministry:

> My Beloved, the mountains,
> and lonely wooded valleys,
> strange islands,
> and resounding rivers,

---

11. Follent, "Negative Experience," 97.

the whistling of love-stirring breezes,
the tranquil night
at the time of the rising dawn,
silent music,
sounding solitude,
the supper that refreshes, and deepens love . . .
There he gave me his breast;
there he taught me a sweet and living knowledge;
and I gave myself to him,
keeping nothing back . . .
Now I occupy my soul
and all my energy in his service . . .
now that my every act is love. [12]

John's colleague too, Teresa of Avila, is emphatic: "All the soul's concern is taken up with how to please Him more and how or where it will show Him the love it bears Him. This is the reason for prayer, my daughters, the purpose of the spiritual marriage: the birth always of good works, good works."[13] The mystical must lead to the prophetic. Recalling the story of Martha and Mary, she calls for an integration of action with contemplation: "This I should like us to attain: we should desire and engage in prayer, not for our enjoyment, but for the sake of acquiring this strength which fits us for service."[14]

QUESTIONS FOR TODAY

Becoming Prophets

This world urgently needs prophets that speak out of an encounter with God in solitude. Those on Emmaus Road spoke of "Jesus of Nazareth, who was a prophet mighty in deed and word before God and all the people" (Luke 24:19), and we recall that the prophets of old both spoke the word of God and also embodied or symbolized the word in a dramatic action. The burden of the Old Testament prophets like Elijah was not prediction of the future, but rather declaring God's word into the present situation, naming the idols and illusions of contemporary society: forthtelling rather than

---

12. John of the Cross, *Collected Works*, 473–75.
13. Teresa of Avila (trans. Kavanaugh and Rodriguez), *Interior Castle*, 189, 190.
14. Teresa of Avila (trans. Peers), *Interior Castle*, 148. See also Bryant, *Journey to the Centre*.

fore-telling. Walter Brueggemann in his classic *The Prophetic Imagination* tells us that the role of the prophet is to envision an alternative consciousness, and to open up for people a different vision of things: to offer a critique of the status quo and, having listened to God and to the cries of the people, to call us back to searing truth and to new creative possibilities. The role of the prophet is to enable an alternative perspective which may be subversive, questioning, compassionate, and which certainly reveals itself in counter-cultural lifestyle and political choices.[15] Jim Wallis puts it: "Prophetic spirituality will always fundamentally challenge the system at its roots and offer genuine alternatives based on values from our truest religious, cultural and political traditions."[16] Liberation theologians Casaldaliga and Vigil ask:

> What path will you take to heaven, other than earth?
> For whom will you go to Carmel if you go up and don't come down?

They go on:

> There is no way to go to heaven except by the earth. Only in history can we welcome and hope for and make the Reign. If we do not take on the responsibilities of our age, in our daily lives of living and working together, struggling and celebrating, politics and faith—what mission are we taking on? What call are we answering? How are we collaborating in God's work? . . .
>
> Human Jacob's ladders, caught up in Jesus' own *kenosis*, we have to "go up" to God and "come down" to human beings, in an unending ebb and flow of contemplation and action, of self-giving and service, of spirit and matter. While we have time.[17]

In the interplay between the mystical and prophetic, we need do more than take another look at an alternating balance in our lives between action and contemplation, between struggle and silence. The greatest challenge is to be contemplatives *in* action: to bring a contemplative listening discerning heart into the very midst of situations of suffering and confusion. Casaldaliga and Vigil put it:

> We are called to live contemplation in liberative activity, decoding surroundings made up of grace and sin, light and shade, justice

---

15. There is a scholarly debate about the nature of Jesus as prophet. Wright, *Victory of God*, sees Jesus as an apocalyptic prophet who embodies the very presence of Israel's God; Sanders, *Historical Figure of Jesus*, sees Jesus as one of a series of Jewish eschatological prophets.

16. Wallis, *Soul of Politics*, 38, 47.

17. Casaldaliga and Vigil, *Spirituality of Liberation*, xxii, xxiii

and injustice, peace and violence, discovering in this historical process the presence of the Wind that blows where it will . . . in the wail of a child, or in the full-throated cry of a people, we try to listen to God . . .[18]

Voices from Mount Carmel challenge us to precisely this.

Handling Stress

We noticed in the story of Elijah how he sometimes learned the hard way about this, and made himself vulnerable to stress in its different forms—external pressures and internal struggles. During the pandemic people have faced stress and strain in different ways. Parents juggling home-schooling of boisterous children while working from home at the same time have faced physical, spiritual and emotional exhaustion. Stress has manifested itself in fracturing relationships, in insomnia, lack of motivation, loss of confidence—all undermining mental health. A survey by the Office for National Statistics made at the start of the first national lockdown showed that half the adult UK population—some 25 million people—reported that they were experiencing high levels of anxiety.[19] And on the other hand, many have actually welcomed an enforced furlough from the daily grind of work: burnout has turned to catchup, life slows down and many have found themselves receiving an unexpected gift of time and space with its potential for healing and restoration.

We have much to learn from the humanity of Elijah and the ways he ultimately found peace. What strikes you most from Elijah's experience? Albert picks up on the theme of striking a balance between competing demands in our lives. A starting point is periodically to review the rhythm and pace of our lives. Survey the last three days of your life, and note down how many hours each day were given to sleep, eating, prayer, study/ learning, recreation/ entertainment, exercise, responding to needs or helping others. Set your findings side by side as you compare the days. What do you notice?

One cause of stress in a time of pandemic has been an incessant flow towards us of depressing or anxious thoughts. The message of John of the Cross about letting go—saying *nada nada nada* to things clamoring to get

---

18. Casaldaliga and Vigil, *Spirituality of Liberation*, 103.
19. Quoted in McKenna, "Stress," 61.

our attention—suggests to us a strategy for rejecting negative thoughts that bombard us. When we find ourselves in the valley we must repeatedly refocus and decisively re-orient ourselves towards the summit and make the ascent of Mount Carmel, however difficult. As Paul puts it: "Finally, beloved, whatever is true, whatever is honorable, whatever is just, whatever is pure, whatever is pleasing, whatever is commendable, if there is any excellence and if there is anything worthy of praise, think about *these* things" (Phil 4: 8).

As we will discover on the Galilean mountains, we can indeed discover a healing and uniting vision in prayer that motivates and sustains us for courageous mission. But next we are summoned to the sacred slopes of Zion, where we will find our heart's true home.

FOR PERSONAL REFLECTION

1. What lessons can you apply from Elijah's experience to your own situation?
2. Take another look at the four pairs of commitments considered by St Albert. What do they say to your lifestyle? Do you need to make any changes?
3. John of the Cross beckons us up Mount Carmel by a pathway of detachment and letting go—that might be the experience of darkness and undoing—so we can reach a new spaciousness of soul symbolized by the summit. How does this resonate with your own spiritual journey?
4. What strategies do you have in order to respond to stress? Do they need to be revisited?
5. In what ways is your life that of a mystic or that of a prophet? Can you be both at the same time—a "contemplative in action"?
6. What situations around you cry out for a prophet's voice? What might you say?

4

Zion
Longing for Fulfilment

> *He fulfils the desire of all who fear him;*
> *he also hears their cry, and saves them. (Ps 145:19)*

BOUNDED BY THE KIDRON valley to the east, Hinnom valley to the south, and Tyropoeon valley to the west, it started inconspicuously enough but became a symbol of humanity's greatest longing. Originally this served as the threshing floor of Arunah the Jebusite, exposed to the elements and catching wind separating wheat from chaff (2 Sam 24). Maybe it was also a high place for Jebusite worship to the deity mentioned, say 2000BC, in the mysterious encounter related in Genesis: "King Melchizedek of Salem brought out bread and wine; he was priest of God Most High. He blessed him and said, 'Blessed be Abram by God Most High, *El Elyon*, maker of heaven and earth'" (14:18,19). The tale of Abraham's binding of Isaac on Mount Moriah (Gen 22) is located here. At some point it gained the name Zion—this means "thirsty place," fitting for the locus of humanity's deepest yearnings, as the psalmist eloquently expresses:

> As a deer longs for flowing streams,
> so my soul longs for you, O God.
> My soul thirsts for God, for the living God.
> When shall I come and behold the face of God?

Zion

My tears have been my food day and night,
while people say to me continually, "Where is your God?"

These things I remember, as I pour out my soul:
how I went with the throng,
and led them in procession to the house of God,
with glad shouts and songs of thanksgiving,
a multitude keeping festival . . .
Hope in God; for I shall again praise him, my help and my God.
(Ps 42)

How lovely is your dwelling place, O LORD of hosts!
My soul longs, indeed it faints for the courts of the LORD;
my heart and my flesh sing for joy to the living God.

Even the sparrow finds a home, and the swallow a nest for herself,
where she may lay her young, at your altars, O LORD of hosts,
my King and my God.
Happy are those who live in your house, ever singing your praise.

Happy are those whose strength is in you,
in whose heart are the highways to Zion . . .
They go from strength to strength;
the God of gods will be seen in Zion. (Ps 84)

In this chapter as we listen to the voices of Mount Zion one theme, like a stream, will keep bubbling up: humanity's yearning for Zion externalizes and represents people's ache for God, our spiritual desire, the craving of the soul for something more. Because Zion is of special significance to all three monotheistic religions, we will hear two voices from each tradition: Jewish longings for Zion, as well as Muslim and Christian voices.

JEWISH VOICES

The First Temple

After David establishes Jerusalem as his religious and political capital, God himself comes to live on Mount Zion, in the biblical perspective. From the Holy of Holies, the innermost sanctuary in the Temple built by Solomon atop the Ophel Ridge in about 970BC, the Ark of the Covenant, bearing the Ten Commandments on two tablets of stone, radiates a circle of holiness.

There is a dramatic account of the building of this first Temple in 2 Chronicles 2–4 and the story of its dedication is told in 2 Chronicles 5–7.

Later, after the disappearance of the Ark, the Holy of Holies becomes a divine void, the primordial sacred space. The holy place is to be approached with awe, fear and trembling—only the purified priest can draw near. The "Holiness Code" (Lev 17–26) directs priest and people on the proper accession to the sanctuary, with its oft-repeated divine injunction: "Be holy, as I am holy" (Lev 11:44,45 cf. 1 Pet 1:15,16). The psalms celebrate Zion and Jerusalem as "the holy place": "Who may ascend the hill of the Lord? Who may stand in his holy place? The one who has clean hands and a pure heart ..." (Ps 24:2). Psalm 46 proclaims Jerusalem "the city of God, the holy place where the Most High dwells." The Temple itself was not a gathering place for a congregation, like a church building. They worshipped outside the building in the courts. The building itself was understood as a residence for the Divine, an earthly dwelling place where God sets his presence.

The First Temple lasted from 970BC to 586BC when it was destroyed by the Babylonians and the Jerusalemites were taken into exile.

The Second Temple

They returned 70 years later and in 516BC work commenced immediately on rebuilding it: the Second Temple arose from the ashes of the first. The story is told in the books of Ezra, Nehemiah and Haggai. At the time of Jesus Herod was completing his stunning restoration of the Second Temple. Herod flattened the top of the mount by laying down a vast platform supported by vaults and retaining walls, of which the Western Wall (Wailing Wall) is a surviving remnant.[1] Jewish historian Josephus tells us that the massive Temple building was constructed in white marble shimmering in the bright sunlight and dazzling onlookers. The glistening stone with its gold decorations made the place radiant and incandescent each morning as the bright Middle Eastern sun rose in the east behind the Mount of Olives opposite. All were overwhelmed by the beauty of the new temple, and its seeming permanence, as faithful Jews made a thrice-yearly pilgrimage to worship there at Passover (*Pesach*), Pentecost (*Shavuot*) and Tabernacles (*Succoth*).

---

1. Even today, the pilgrim encounters a warning sign, erected by the Chief Rabbinate of Israel, at the last remnant of the Second Temple: "You are approaching the holy site of the Western Wall, where the Divine Presence always rests."

Zion

The Second Temple was utterly destroyed in 70AD by Roman forces under Titus.[2]

From the time of its destruction and up to the present, Mount Zion has been the focus of Jewish longing and abiding symbol of the Divine.[3] The very last words of the traditional Seder (Passover meal) are "next year in Jerusalem"—remembrances of past blessings are transposed to future hope. The 14th blessing of the *Amidah*, which is the core of every Jewish worship service and recited three times daily, prays for the return of the divine *shekinah* glory:

> Have mercy and return to Jerusalem, Your city.
> May Your presence dwell there as You have promised.
> Build it now, in our days and for all time.
> Re-establish there the majesty of David, Your servant.
> Praised are You Adonai, who builds Jerusalem.[4]

The desire in the Jewish soul for God is expressed in an aching for a return to Zion.

YEHUDA HALEVI (1075–1141)—physician and religious philosopher regarded as the greatest of all the medieval Hebrew poets, his prayers finding their way into the Jewish liturgy—pens one of the most intense expressions of this longing. Born in Toledo, Spain, Yehuda's lifetime of longing for Zion was crowned by his pilgrimage to the Holy Land in 1141, when he finally set eyes on the sacred mount he had been dreaming about for more than sixty years, and he died soon after.

> Zion! Do you wonder how and where your captives
> Are now, and if they think of you, the far-flocked remnants?
> From north and south, east, west, and all directions,
> Near and far, they send their greetings
> As I send mine, captured by my longings
> To weep like Hermon's dew upon your mountains.

---

2. Recent archaeology has revealed the stunning flight of steps (Hulda Steps) by which people entered the Temple area, the monumental steps and bridge across the Tyropoeon Valley used by the clergy (Robinson's Arch), a first century street with temple shops, mikveh or ritual baths used by pilgrims; fragments of the Second Temple, as the Romans cast down the blocks of walls, were found in the valley below.

3. Last century Zionism reached its climax in the occupation of the Temple Mount by the Israelis in 1967. Today there is a mounting campaign for the building of the third Temple.

4. Quoted by Upbin, "Praying for Jerusalem," third paragraph.

Voices from the Mountains

Mourning your lowliness, I am the wail of jackals;
Dreaming your sons' return, the song of lute strings . . .
You He illumines
Not with the sun, or moon, or stars, but with the rays
Of His own glory. Gladly I would choose
To pour my soul out where your chosen ones
Stood in a downpour of God's effluence.
You are the throne of the Lord, His royal house –
How then are slaves enthroned in your lords' houses?
If only I could wander past the way points
Where God appeared to your appointed and your seers,
And, flying to you with a bird's wings,
Shake woeful head, remembering the throes
Of your dismemberment, my face
Pressed to your earth, cherishing its soil and stones . . .
    Your very air's alive with souls;
Your earth breathes incense and your rivers
Run with balm. I would rejoice
To walk with my bare feet, in tatters,
Upon the ruins of your Sanctuaries,
In which, before it was removed from us,
The Holy Ark stood guarded by its Cherubs
Posted at the innermost of chambers . . .
    Zion! God's love, combined with Beauty's grace,
Has bound to you the souls of all Your friends,
So that they joy when you're at peace
And weep when you're all wounds and wilderness.
Imprisoned, they yearn for you, each from his place
Turning to bow in prayer to your gates—
Your many flocks, dispersed to distant hills
Yet ever mindful of their vows
To re-ascend to you and reach your heights,
As the palm tree, rising above all else,
Is scaled by the bold climber. Who compares
To you? Not ancient Babylon, nor Greece:
What are all their empty oracles
Beside your Prophets and the breastplates of your priests?
The heathen kingdoms lapse, collapse, and pass,
But you remain forever, crowned for the ages.
God makes His home in you: Blessed are those
Who dwell with Him, residing in your courts.
Blessed is he who comes, and waits, and sees
The rising sun illuminate your dawns,

Zion

In which your steadfast share the happiness
Of your lost Youth, restored as it once was.[5]

MOSES MAIMONIDES (1138–1204), a contemporary of Halevi, was an important medieval Jewish scholar and prolific writer, hailed as the "second Moses" by his followers. Born in Spain, after a significant visit to the Holy Land in 1165, he moved to Egypt, serving as personal physician to Saladin. His monumental work *The Guide for the Perplexed* is not only a milestone in Jewish philosophy but also influenced the wider world during that period: Christian leaders, such as Thomas Aquinas, called him "Rabbi Moses." Living in the religious melting pot of North Africa, Maimonides brought together four cultures—Greco-Roman, Arab, Jewish, and Western—and he endures as one of the most influential religious philosophers of the intellectual world.

He had a strong conviction that the divine presence remained on Zion, despite the destruction of the temple. An intriguing line in his writing relates his visit to the Holy City in 1165 "where I entered the great holy house."[6] Did he pray within the Dome of the Rock which stands on the crest of the holy hill? He later wrote: "When a person enters the Temple, certain emotions are produced in him; and obstinate hearts are softened and humbled."[7] On his move to Egypt, he produced detailed descriptions of the Temple and even a sketch, and remains a vital source for those interested even today in Temple ritual.[8] Maybe he had in mind the concentric zones of the former Temple when he wrote of humanity's longing for God by means of an allegory:

> A King is in his palace, and all his subjects are partly in the country, and partly abroad. Of the former, some have their backs turned towards the King's palace, and their faces in another direction; and some are desirous and zealous to go to the palace, seeking "to inquire in his temple," and to minister before him, but have not yet seen even the face of the wall of the house. Of those that desire to go to the palace, some reach it, and go round about in search of the entrance gate; others have passed through the gate, and walk about in the ante-chamber; and others have succeeded

---

5. Halkin, *Yehuda Halevi*. For Halevi's journey to the Holy Land see. Scheindlin, *Song of the Distant Dove*.

6. Note attached to commentary on Mishnaic tractate "Rosh Hashana," translation by Davidson, *Moses Maimonides*.

7. Maimonides, *Guide for the Perplexed*, 274 (Part 3:XLV).

8. Frenkel, "Temple Mount," 349.

in entering into the inner part of the palace, and being in the same room with the King in the royal palace. But even the latter do not immediately on entering the palace see the King, or speak to him; for, after having entered the inner part of the palace, another effort is required before they can stand before the King—at a distance, or close by—hear his words, or speak to him.

I will now explain the simile which I have made.

The people who are abroad are all those that have no religion, neither one based on speculation nor one received by tradition . . .

Those who are in the country, but have their backs turned towards the King's palace, are those who possess religion, belief, and thought, but happen to hold false doctrines . . . they recede more and more from the royal palace the more they seem to proceed . . .

Those who desire to arrive at the palace, and to enter it, but have never yet seen it, are the mass of religious people; the multitude that observe the divine commandments, but are ignorant.

Those who arrive at the palace, but go round about it, are those who devote themselves exclusively to the study of the practical law; they believe traditionally in true principles of faith, and learn the practical worship of God, but are not trained in philosophical treatment of the principles of the Law, and do not endeavor to establish the truth of their faith by proof.

Those who undertake to investigate the principles of religion, have come into the ante-chamber; and there is no doubt that these can also be divided into different grades.

But those who have succeeded in finding a proof for everything that can be proved, who have a true knowledge of God, so far as a true knowledge can be attained, and are near the truth, wherever an approach to the truth is possible, they have reached the goal, and are in the palace in which the King lives.

My son, so long as you are engaged in studying the Mathematical Sciences and Logic, you belong to those who go round about the palace in search of the gate . . . When you understand Physics, you have entered the hall; and when, after completing the study of Natural Philosophy, you master Metaphysics, you have entered the innermost court, and are with the King in the same palace. You have attained the degree of the wise ones, who include people of different grades of perfection. There are some who direct all their mind toward the attainment of perfection in Metaphysics, devote themselves entirely to God, exclude from their thought every other thing, and employ all their intellectual faculties in the study of the Universe, in order to derive therefrom a proof for the existence of God, and to learn in every possible way how God

> rules all things; they form the class of those who have entered the palace, namely, the class of prophets ...
>
> We exhort those who have attained a knowledge of God, to concentrate all their thoughts in God. This is the worship peculiar to those who have acquired a knowledge of the highest truths; and the more they reflect on Him, and think of Him, the more are they engaged in His worship. The Law distinctly states that the highest kind of worship is only possible after the acquisition of the knowledge of God. For it is said, "To love the Lord your God, and to serve Him with all your heart and with all your soul" (Deut 11:13): our love of God is identical with our knowledge of Him.
>
> It must be our aim, after having acquired the knowledge of God, to deliver ourselves up to Him, and to have our hearts constantly filled with longing after Him. We accomplish this generally by seclusion and retirement.
>
> God is near to all who call Him, if we call Him in truth, and turn to Him. He is found by everyone who seeks Him, if we always go towards Him, and never go astray. Amen.[9]

As Maimonides develops the theme of longing for God through this allegory he invites the reader to locate himself or herself: where am I in my relationship with God? Have I passed through the gate towards the inner courts? Have I reached the ante-chamber of the King's palace or ever glimpsed the innermost throne-room? We notice that Maimonides is concerned to balance the needs of both heart and mind, the workings of both intellect and soul in humanity's quest for the Divine.

ISLAMIC VOICES

After the building on the sacred crest of the astonishing Islamic octagonal structure the Dome of the Rock in 691, Zion became known in Islamic circles as *Al Haram esh-Sharif,* the Noble Sanctuary. Now it was the third most holiest place in Islam after Mecca and Medina, being the site of Mohammed's night-time ascent into heaven, when he was entrusted with the five-fold daily prayer, the *salat*. The great Al-Aqsa mosque was built soon afterwards, and the mountain became a magnet for Muslims seeking a deeper encounter with God.

---

9. Maimonides, *Guide for the Perplexed,* 290–292 (Part 3: LI). Adapted for inclusive language.

RABA'A (713–801) was a great female Sufi mystic born in the Iraqi city of Basra who crossed the deserts to reach Jerusalem. Her tomb, next to the Mosque of the Ascension atop the Mount of Olives, looks out to the Haram opposite. A Sufi poet, singer, and mystic, Raba'a pioneered the daring use of the language of intimacy for the Divine, famously developed by Rumi. God was for her the only Beloved—stunningly beautiful herself and frequently pursued by would-be lovers, she consecrated herself body and soul to God. She had been enslaved until the man who purchased her saw light radiating around her one evening while she was kneeling in prayer. Raba'a wrote poems describing her unquenchable love for God. Camille Adams Helminski explains her significance:

> As the mystical side of Islam developed, it was a woman who first expressed the relationship with the Divine in a language we have come to recognize as specifically Sufic by referring to God as the Beloved. Raba'a was the first human being to speak of the realities of Sufism with a language that anyone could understand. Though she experienced many difficulties in her early years, Raba'a's starting point was neither a fear of hell nor a desire for paradise, but only love. "God is God", she said, "for this I love God . . . not because of any gifts, but for Himself." Her aim was to melt her being in God. According to her, one could find God by turning within oneself.[10]

Let's listen to her voice singing to us across the centuries:

> Cup, Wine and Friend make three:
> And I, thirsty with love, am Four . . .
> The Cupbearer hands to each, one after another
> The cup of unending joy:
> If I look, it's Him I am looking for;
> And if I arrive, then He is my eyes.
> Don't blame me if I am in love with His beauty . . . [11]

Her poems reveal an intensity of spiritual desire, sometimes expressed in physical terms:

> My peace, brothers, is in my aloneness
> Because my Beloved is alone with me there—always.
> I've found nothing to equal His love,
> That love which harrows the sands of my desert.

10. Helminski, *Women of Sufism*.
11. Upton, *Doorkeeper of the Heart*, 3.

Zion

If I die of desire, and He is still unsatisfied—
That sorrow has no end.[12]

O God, the stars are shining;
All eyes have closed in sleep:
The kings have locked their doors.
Each lover is alone, in secret, with the one he loves.
And I am here too: hidden from all of them—
With You.[13]

In love, nothing exists between breast and Breast.
Speech is born out of longing.
True description from the real taste.
The one who tastes, knows;
The one who explains, lies.[14]

Raba'a finds God as she listens to the sounds of creation:

O God,
Whenever I listen to the voice of anything You have made—
The rustling of the trees
The trickling of water
The cries of birds
The flickering of shadow
The roar of the wind
The song of the thunder,
I hear it saying:

God is One!
Nothing can be compared with God![15]

Raba'a's desire for God expresses itself in a litany of divine names:

My Joy
My Hunger
My Shelter
My Friend
My Food for the Journey
My Journey's End

12. Upton, *Doorkeeper of the Heart*, 9.
13. Upton, *Doorkeeper of the Heart*, 66.
14. Upton, *Doorkeeper of the Heart*, 31.
15. Upton, *Doorkeeper of the Heart*, 58.

Voices from the Mountains

> You are my breath,
> My hope,
> My companion,
> My craving,
> My abundant wealth...
> My Life, my Love...
> O Captain of my Heart,
> Radiant Eye of Yearning in my breast...
> Be satisfied with me, Love
> And I am satisfied. [16]

Referring to the Sufi *dhikr* practice of the Remembrance of God—repetition of the divine names accompanied by bodily swaying—she writes:

> Your hope in my heart is the rarest treasure
> Your Name on my tongue is the sweetest word
> My choicest hours
> Are the hours I spend with You—
> O God, I can't live in this world
> Without remembering You.[17]

> O God...
> Give the goods of this world to Your enemies—
> Give the treasures of Paradise to Your friends—
> But as for me—You are all I need.[18]

So Raba'a ascends the holy mount, but a question remains:

> "Raba'a—Raba'a—how did you climb so high?"
> "I did it by saying:
>   'Let me hide in You
>   From everything that distracts me from You,
>   From everything that comes in my way
>   When I want to run to You.'"[19]

ABU HAMED AL-GHAZALI (1058–1111) is Islam's greatest scholar and mystic, but his voice is little heard in the West. Renard affirms "He is among the towering figures of Islamic thought in general and of the literature of

---

16. Upton, *Doorkeeper of the Heart*, 57.
17. Upton, *Doorkeeper of the Heart*, 51.
18. Upton, *Doorkeeper of the Heart*, 47.
19. Upton, *Doorkeeper of the Heart*, 55.

spirituality in particular."[20] He was developing a distinguished career as professor at a madrasa in Baghdad when in 1095 he underwent a spiritual crisis—he questioned the inherited scholastic and theoretical understandings of Islamic theology and longed for something experiential, personal and transformative. He abandoned his teaching career and left Baghdad on the pretext of going on pilgrimage to Mecca but, journeying via Damascus, he sojourned for a year instead in Jerusalem. Al-Ghazali came to the Holy City as a seeker, feeling spiritually empty and on a quest for a real encounter with the Divine. He tells his story in his autobiography. While in Baghdad, he says,

> I incessantly vacillated between the contending pull of worldly desires and the appeals of the afterlife for about six months, starting with Rajab of the year 488 (July, 1095AD) . . .
>
> Then, when I perceived my powerlessness, and when my capacity to make a choice had completely collapsed, I had recourse to God Most High as does a hard pressed man who has no way out of his difficulty. And I was answered by Him Who "answers the needy man when he calls on Him", and He made it easy for my heart to turn away from fame and fortune, family, children, and associates. I announced that I had resolved to leave . . .
>
> Then I entered Damascus and resided there for nearly two years. My only occupation was seclusion and solitude and spiritual exercise and combat with a view to devoting myself to the purification of my soul and the cultivation of virtues and cleansing my heart for the remembrance of God Most High, in the way I had learned from the writings of the Sufis. I used to pray in seclusion for a time in the Mosque, mounting to its minaret for the whole day and shutting myself in. Then I traveled from Damascus to Jerusalem, where I would go daily into the Dome of the Rock and shut myself in.[21]

In 1095–1096 Al-Ghazali lived on the Haram itself, a stone's throw from the awesome Dome of the Rock. He lodged in a room beneath the dome of the Gate of Mercy, part of the Golden Gate itself. Times of solitude at the Rock alternated with times of learning with Sufis. The first Sufis had come to Jerusalem in the early centuries of Islam from the eastern provinces of the Islamic world and by Al-Ghazali's time the city was growing into an important a Sufi center, with a number of *tariqas* or schools of wisdom

20. Renard, *Knowledge of God*, 45.
21. Al-Ghazali, *Deliverance from Error*, 20.

on the edge of the Haram.[22] Inspired by their first-hand experience of the mystic way, he reflected later:

> In the course of those periods of solitude things impossible to enumerate or detail in depth were disclosed to me. This much I shall mention, that profit may be derived from it: I knew with certainty that the Sufis are those who uniquely follow the way to God Most High, their mode of life is the best of all, their way the most direct of ways, and their ethic the purest. Indeed, were one to combine the insight of the intellectuals, the wisdom of the wise, and the lore of scholars versed in the mysteries of revelation in order to change a single item of Sufi conduct and ethic and to replace it with something better, no way to do so would be found! For all their motions and quiescences, exterior and interior, are learned from the light of the niche of prophecy. And beyond the light of prophecy there is no light on earth from which illumination can be obtained. In general, how can we describe such a way as this? Its purity—the first of its requirements—is the total purification of the heart from everything other than God Most High. Its key, which is analogous to the beginning of the Prayer, is the utter absorption of the heart in the remembrance of God.[23]

What did he discover on the holy mountain? Al-Ghazali embodied his discoveries on the Noble Sanctuary in a major work *The Revival of Religious Sciences* written on the mount. This went on to become the most influential work on ethics in Islamic history and the most frequently read Islamic book after the Qur'an. It brings together orthodox Sunni theology and Sufi mysticism in a useful, comprehensible manner to guide every aspect of Muslim life. It springs from Al-Ghazali's personal spiritual experience and a key theme, resonating with what we have encountered on this holy mountain so far, is that of longing and desire for God:

> We affirm the necessity of longing for God and that the gnostic is compelled to it due to the lights of inner vision in contemplation and following Traditions . . .
>
> Divine matters are infinite and unbounded; to every person only a few are disclosed while infinitely many remain obscure. The gnostic knows that these exist and are known to God. We realize that these knowables that elude our comprehension are more numerous than those that are present to us. We yearn incessantly to

---

22. For an introduction to Sufism in Jerusalem past and present see Mayes, *Gateways to the Divine*. See also Nasr, *Islamic Spirituality*; Nicholson, *Mystics of Islam*.

23. Al-Ghazali, *Deliverance from Error*, 21.

Zion

acquire some primary, as-yet-unattained knowledge of all remaining things knowable and which we know not in the least, either clearly or even dimly...

We remain constantly aware that something in the divine beauty and grandeur remains irreducibly inexplicable. Our longing can never be stilled—but we yearn to consummate our union by arriving at the root of union. For this reason we discover pleasurable longing in which no pain appears. And it is very probable that the twin graces of disclosure and contemplation continue indefinitely, just as bliss and pleasure keep increasing forever and ever.[24]

Living on the site of Zion so closely associated with David, Al-Ghazali recalls:

> In the Traditions of David, God is reported to have said, "O David, tell the inhabitants of My earth, 'I am a loving friend to whomever loves Me. I keep company with the one who sits with Me. I am close to the one who keeps mention of Me close to himself. I am the companion of the one who companions Me... You do not love Me—and I know this for a certainty from your heart—without My taking you to Myself and I love you with such a love as none of My creation can surpass. You who search for Me in truth shall find Me ... O dweller on earth, cast aside the vanities to which you cling and come close to My munificence, My companionship and My converse! Be intimate with Me and I will be so with you and I will rush to love you... the hearts of those who yearn I created from My own light and I have given them bliss in My glory.'"[25]

Al-Ghazali develops Raba'a's theme of intimacy, and helps to lay a foundation for an Islamic mysticism—later perfected by Rumi—that delights in erotic language:

> On the authority of one of the pious ancestors, it is reported that God inspired one of the truthful with the following words, "I have certain servants who love Me and I love them. They yearn for Me and I for them." He asked, "O Lord! What distinguishing marks do these people have?" God said, "They watch over the shadows by day as a tender herdsman watches over his sheep. They long for the sun to set as a bird longs for its nest at dusk. When the night hides them and shadows mingle and dark spreads out its coverings and makes ready the beds and every lover is alone with his beloved,

---

24. Al-Ghazali, *Love, Longing and Contentment*, 88–90.
25. Al-Ghazali, *Love, Longing and Contentment*, 91–92.

they direct their steps toward Me and raise up their faces before Me, and they whisper confidences to Me in My own speech and cajole Me for My beneficence . . . I shall draw My face close unto them; and to whom I draw near, who will be privy to what I shall give him?"[26]

After his transformative time on Zion, Al-Ghazali had come to a new sense of his vocation and purpose and, after a visit to Medina and Mecca in 1096, he went to Persia to spend the next several years in seclusion, teaching in the Sufi monastery that he had built. Later, he resumed his teaching work more fully, inspired and fortified by his times of stillness and solitude.

CHRISTIAN VOICES

The Third Temple

Jesus foretold the destruction of the Temple. [27]

> As he came out of the temple, one of his disciples said to him, "Look, Teacher, what large stones and what large buildings!" Then Jesus said to him, "Do you see these great buildings? Not one stone will be left here upon another; all will be thrown down" (Mark 13:1,2).

In the Temple Jesus saw his vocation and destiny, more clearly than ever before, in terms of both demolition and rebuilding. Jesus, it seems, had a stunningly outrageous understanding of his calling and identity. He was to be the new locus of the Divine! For a thousand years the Divine had been thought to reside in the temple, represented there first of all, by the Ark of the Covenant placed in the Holy of Holies. "See, something greater than Solomon is here" (Matt 12:42). Jesus points to himself, to his very body, as the place where God is now to be discovered (John 2:22). But this is no painless theophany: there is to be a violent desecration and destruction of the temple of his body, and it is to be laid in ruins, before something new and mysterious is to arise. At the death of Jesus, the heavy veil that separated the Holy of Holies from the nave was torn in two, "from top to bottom" (Matt 27:51).

---

26. Al-Ghazali, *Love, Longing and Contentment*, 92–93.

27. Jesus' prophetic action we call the "Cleansing of the Temple"—the casting down of traders' tables crashing to the ground—had vividly enacted its demise. Wright, *Jesus and the Victory of God*.

The Fourth Temple

The Christian community understands itself as the Body of Christ and as the fourth and final Temple. This is true both corporately—and individually—my own body is a temple for God to dwell in:

> Do you not know that you are God's temple and that God's Spirit dwells in you? If anyone destroys God's temple, God will destroy that person. For God's temple is holy, and you are that temple. (1 Cor 3: 16,17)

> The body is meant ... for the Lord, and the Lord for the body. And God raised the Lord and will also raise us by his power ... do you not know that your body is a temple and sanctuary of the Holy Spirit within you, which you have from God, and that you are not your own? For you were bought with a price; therefore glorify God in your body. (1 Cor 6:19–20)

The church is like a building site, a work in progress. Paul says "we are *being built*"—it is going on now:

> So then you are no longer strangers and aliens, but you are citizens with the saints and also members of the household of God, built upon the foundation of the apostles and prophets, with Christ Jesus himself as the cornerstone. In him the whole structure is joined together and grows into a holy temple in the Lord; in whom *you also are being built* together spiritually into a dwelling-place for God. (Eph 2:19–22)

Peter develops this idea of a present-day building of the Temple too:

> Come to him, a living stone, though rejected by mortals yet chosen and precious in God's sight, and like living stones, *you yourselves are being built* into a spiritual house, to be a holy priesthood, to offer spiritual sacrifices acceptable to God through Jesus Christ ... You are a chosen race, a royal priesthood, a holy nation, God's own people, in order that you may proclaim the mighty acts of him who called you out of darkness into his marvelous light (1 Pet 2:4–9).

SOPHRONIUS (560–638), Jerusalem's patriarch in the seventh century, was widely traveled throughout the Middle East, visiting such places as Constantinople and Alexandria, but for him only one place on earth radiated the saving presence of God. In his poem *Anacreonticon 20* he gives voice to his yearning for the physical Zion:

> Holy City of God,
> Jerusalem, how I long to stand
> even now at your gates,
> and go in, rejoicing!
>   A divine longing for holy Salem
> presses upon me insistently . . .
>   Hail, Zion, radiant Sun of the universe!
> Night and day I long and yearn for thee.[28]

Christians had begun in the fourth century to call Jerusalem's south western hill by the name of Zion, erecting important churches there in memory of the Last Supper and Pentecost. Christians did not return to the original holy mount until the Crusaders came to Jerusalem in 1099. Their mission was to safeguard routes of access to the Holy Sepulcher (Church of the Resurrection), but they did not base themselves there but on the Temple Mount, becoming known as the Knights Templar.[29] Erecting a cross on the top, they called the Dome of the Rock *Templum Domini* and the Al-Aqsa mosque was converted into their headquarters.

BERNARD OF CLAIRVAUX (1090–1153), founder of Cistercian monasticism, was asked by Pope Eugene III to preach in support of a second crusade. Some of his sermon *In Praise of the New Knighthood* glorifying the Crusades, makes for uncomfortable reading, but we can allow ourselves to hear his glorifying of the holy mountain of Zion:

> Hail, holy city, sanctified as His temple [by] the Most High . . .
>   Hail, city of the Great King, out of which new and happy wonders have come in virtually all times since the creation for the benefit of the world.
>   Hail, mistress of the nations, leader of the provinces, property of the patriarchs, mother of the prophets and apostles, cradle of the faith, glory of the Christian people . . .
>   Hail, promised land, that formerly flowed with milk and honey solely for your inhabitants, now you offer to the whole world the life-sustaining food that is the means of salvation.

---

28. Wilkinson, *Jerusalem Pilgrims*, 157.

29. The Knights Hospitaller were located closer to the Sepulcher, ministering to sick and wounded pilgrims.

Zion

> You are a good land, I say, that received in your most fertile womb a heavenly seed from the treasure-chest of the Father's heart
>
> ...
>
> Having happily banqueted on and most satisfyingly partaken of the great quantity of your sweetness, those who have seen you proclaim everywhere the memory of your abundant sweetness, and they talk of the magnificence of your glory to those who have not seen you, even to the ends of the earth ... "Glorious things are spoken of thee, O city of God."[30]

BERNARD OF CLUNY (1100–1150), a contemporary only too aware of the fragility of human life here below, knew the paradox that the City of Peace has often been a battlefield. Bernard of Cluny transposes earthly longings for the Holy City into a desire for heaven. Jerusalem, as in the book of Revelation, becomes a symbol of eternity:

> And I saw the holy city, the new Jerusalem, coming down out of heaven from God, prepared as a bride adorned for her husband.
> And I heard a loud voice from the throne saying,
> "See, the home of God is among mortals.
> He will dwell with them; they will be his peoples,
> and God himself will be with them;
> he will wipe every tear from their eyes.
> Death will be no more;
> mourning and crying and pain will be no more,
> for the first things have passed away."
> And the one who was seated on the throne said,
> "See, I am making all things new." (Rev 21:3–5).

Bernard catches this awesome vision in which humanity's deepest longings and yearnings are forever fulfilled, and he sings his heart out:

> Jerusalem the golden with milk and honey blest,
> Beneath thy contemplation sink heart and voice oppressed.
> I know not, oh, I know not what joys await us there,
> What radiancy of glory, what bliss beyond compare.
>
> They stand, those halls of Sion, all jubilant with song,
> And bright with many an Angel, and all the Martyr throng;
> The Prince is ever in them, the daylight is serene;
> The pastures of the blessed are decked in glorious sheen.

---

30. Barber and Bate, *Templars*, 226–27.

There is the throne of David; and there, from care released,
The shout of them that triumph, the song of them that feast;
And they, who with their Leader have conquered in the fight,
For ever and for ever are clad in robes of white.

O sweet and blessed country the home of God's elect!
O sweet and blessed country that eager hearts expect!
Jesu, in mercy bring us to that dear land of rest;
Who art, with God the Father and Spirit, ever Blest.[31]

QUESTIONS FOR TODAY

In this chapter we have noticed how humanity's deepest longings for the Divine become focused on holy mountains like Zion, concentrated with an intensity of devotion at holy places. Many have become what the Celtic tradition calls "thin places", where the veil between heaven and earth, between the human and divine is easily crossed—where there is often, to this day, a palpable sense of God's presence, deepened by the prayers of the centuries in these holy places, where pilgrims sense what Otto called "the numinous" in his classic work *A Sense of the Holy*.

The pandemic causes us to rethink our ideas of holy places. Those working in hospitals and especially in intensive care units describe them not only as a battlefield and but also as a sacred place, holy ground where they have witnessed close-up both the mystery of healing and the passing of souls to another life. Where indeed do we find God? Where should we be looking for Christ? Can it be that we can encounter him, not only in holy rocks and hills but also in the broken lives of the oppressed and hurting? Christ's parable invites us to discern his features in the faces of those who suffer:

> The King will say to those at his right hand, 'Come, you that are blessed by my Father; inherit the kingdom prepared for you from the foundation of the world, for I was hungry and you gave me food, I was thirsty and you gave me something to drink, I was a stranger and you welcomed me in, I was naked and you gave me clothing, I was sick and you took care of me, I was in prison and you visited me . . . Truly I tell you, just as you did it to one of the least of those who are members of my family, you did for me.' (Matt. 25:34–36, 40)

31. Translated by John Mason Neale.

Zion

The life of Jesus redefines holiness. The incarnation redefines the holy. Now we touch the holy God in his incarnate life in Jesus. We see the holy, in Jesus, in the dirt of a Bethlehem stable, in the simplicity and poverty of Galilee, in the heartache and longing of his tears on the Mount of Olives, in the pain and isolation of Calvary, in the mystery of Easter—there, in these "holy places" God's presence is to be discovered and welcomed. Jesus invites us to find him in "these brothers and sisters of mine" who are hungry, broken, sick, estranged. The incarnation overturns the traditional dichotomy between sacred and secular, the divide between "holy" and "unholy." It challenges us to glimpse the Divine in the dust, and to be alert to God's presence in the broken.[32] It alerts us to the possibility that Christ might be close at hand, incognito, waiting to be recognized and greeted. In Christ's parable the question is "Lord, when did we *see* you..?" The question is, where do we see the Divine today, and where do we miss this? Our prayer might echo that of Bartimeus: "Lord, that I may see!" (Mark 10:51). We can walk with blinkered eye, vision narrowed by routine or personal urgencies; with shut eye, closed by prejudice; with lazy eye, inattentive. Or we may walk with open eye, ready to glimpse God, in holy places and beyond.

There is still a role for holy places in the traditional sense, but only if they do not become idols, and things in themselves to be venerated. The holy places can be powerful reminders of the God who comes to us, markers in the soil of where God has walked. Yes, they can be "sacred spaces" where we can encounter the Divine. But they need to be seen as *clues* as to the type of God we believe in, a passionate and compassionate God who enters fully into our human condition and is close to the broken-hearted. The rocks and churches of the "holy places" testify to a God who empties himself, a dusty and dirty God who involves himself fully in the pain of humanity.

John of Damascus in the eighth century called the holy places "receptacles of divine energy." Maybe we can think of them as not so much as "receptacles" but as places of divine energy in the sense that they can disturb, challenge us, question us. They can stimulate and inspire us in our search for God. They are not ends in themselves but potentially helps on the journey: *signposts* to where Christ may be revealing himself today in human lives caught up into the midst of crisis.[33]

---

32. Liberation theology has opened our eyes to the ways in which God reveals his Kingdom and his presence precisely through the poor: see, for example, Boff, *Jesus Christ Liberator*.

33. I have written elsewhere (Mayes, *Holy Land?*) of how the silver Star of Bethlehem, the focal point of veneration in the Cave of the Nativity marking the birthplace of Jesus,

FOR PERSONAL REFLECTION

1. In this chapter we have heard how seekers externalize their inner longing for the Divine in terms of yearning for a sacred place imbued with divine presence, that can be imagined or visited. What place might represent for you the fulfilment of your heart's longings?
2. Which expressions here of longing for God and for Zion have inspired you the most?
3. In what ways might you identify with Al-Ghazali's quest and spiritual journey?
4. How would you give voice to your longing for the Divine? Maybe you can compose a poem with imagery drawn from this chapter?
5. In this chapter we see the interplay between physicality and spirituality, and how holy places can be a focus for our spiritual longings. What is your experience of holy places? Where do you find them? Has this changed in a time of pandemic?
6. As you reflect on your relationship with God, where would you locate yourself in Maimonides' map of the approach to the King's palace?
7. How can we heighten our awareness of the presence of God in the faces of those who suffer?

---

begins to look more like a compass pointing away from itself, east and west, north and south, for example to the refugee camps a mile way at Dheisheh, Aida and Al-Azzeh.

5

Desert Mountains
Exploring the Terrain of Prayer

> *I will open rivers on the bare heights,*
> *and fountains in the midst of the valleys;*
> *I will make the wilderness a pool of water* (Isa 41:18)

THE VERY WORD "DESERT" may evoke in the imagination scenes of endless arid sand dunes, perhaps a sense of desolation. In fact, as we shall see, the desert becomes a central experience in Christian spirituality, holding in itself the very secrets of prayer, a place of radical exposure to God. Unlike the windswept dunes of Gaza, where monastic life also flourished[1] the Judean wilderness is a rugged mountainous area which became the birthplace and source of ascetic life.

The Judean desert stretches east from the central highlands towards the fault-line scarp of the Great Rift Valley. The pilgrim approaching Jerusalem and the Mount of Olives (at 2700 feet) from Jericho in the Jordan valley near the Dead Sea, the lowest point on earth, must make an ascent of four thousand feet through the Judean desert. Indeed, the word for pilgrim in Hebrew is *aliyah*, meaning "going up" as is echoed in the psalms of ascent: "Jerusalem, built as a city bound firmly together, to which the tribes go up,

---

1. Barsanuphius, John, and Dorotheos in the sixth century.

the tribes of the Lord" (Ps 122); "As the mountains surround Jerusalem so the Lord is round about his people" (Ps 125: 2). Pilgrims find themselves praying "I lift up my eyes to the hills—from where will my help come? My help comes from the LORD, who made heaven and earth" (Ps 121).

The desert is the archetypal liminal place. It is the space between the River and the City. This is a windswept, rocky and rugged wilderness. Mountains rise above sheer limestone cliff walls pock-marked and honey-combed with caves, while chalk hills tower above narrow deeply-incised canyons. The chiseled marl ravines are parchingly dry for much of the year, but in winter, rains from Jerusalem pour through them in torrents force-ful enough to move great boulders, which litter the riverbed. Acacia and juniper trees cling to the cliffs, while hawks circle overhead, Bedouin's goats picking their way precariously over the rocks. By day rock badgers (coneys) scamper amidst the rocks, while at night the howling of hyenas resounds across the canyons. The Judean desert is a place of paradox: rugged grandeur, raw splendor, untamable beauty, threatening yet inviting, affirming yet disturbing, a place of life and death. The desert mountains are wild, exposed places, calling forth authenticity and honesty from the soul. They are eroded places, where the elements of wind and sun and water split rocks and crumble cliffs, symbolizing the brokenness of humanity. They are open places, bespeaking of the vulnerability of the soul. And yet they are awesomely beautiful and inspiring places, reflecting the potentialities of the human spirit.

It was at the edge of these very hills that the Qumran community established itself about 100BC: later producing the *Dead Sea Scrolls,* they sought to model an alternative apocalyptic community awaiting the Redeemer. The desert has always attracted those on the social margin: fugitives, solitaries, outlaws, hermits . . .

The remnants of one monastery are to be found in the upper section of the scary Wadi Og (Wadi Mukelik). In his sixth century account of the discovery of this site as a suitable place of prayer and retreat by Theoctistus and Euthymius, Cyril of Scythopolis gives us a vivid sense of the topography:

> As they passed through the desert they came to a terrifying gorge, extremely steep and impassable. On seeing the place and going round the cliffs above it they found, as if guided by God, a huge and marvelous cave in the northern cliff of the gorge. Not without danger they made the steep ascent and just managed to climb up

to it. Overjoyed as if the cave had been prepared for them by God, they made it their home.[2]

As we turn to the New Testament, we discover that the Gospel actually begins in this very desert of human need: "The beginning of the good news of Jesus Christ, the Son of God. As it is written in the prophet Isaiah: 'See, I am sending my messenger ahead of you, who will prepare your way: the voice of one crying out in the wilderness: Prepare the way of the Lord!'" (Mark 1:1,2). The very landscape and environment embody the text that inspires John the Baptist: "make straight in the desert a highway for our God. Every valley shall be lifted up, and every mountain and hill be made low" (Isa 40: 3,4). John's voice echoes among the rocks and waste-places: "Turn back to God!" The desert, symbolic of humanity's emptiness, becomes the place of salvation, the place of transformation, through John's call to *metanoia*, repentance, a total re-orientation of lives towards God.

Jesus begins his ministry amidst these desert mountains. After his baptism, he is driven by the Spirit into the inner desert: "Then Jesus was led *up* by the Spirit into the wilderness to be tempted by the devil" (Matt 4:1). The account of his temptation goes on "The devil took him to a very high mountain . . ." (Matt 4:8). Jesus discovers these peaks to be places of angels and demons, as Mark puts it succinctly: "He was in the wilderness forty days, tempted by Satan; and he was with the wild beasts; and the angels waited on him" (Mark 1:13). Jesus experiences the desert as a place of conflict, in which he decisively battles with shortcuts to prestige, pride and power. But, most of all, it becomes the place where he learns to discern the Father's voice, and discovers the priorities for his ensuing ministry. Here he learns what was to become the secret of his ministry: "Very truly, I tell you, the Son can do nothing on his own but only what he sees his Father doing . . . The Father loves the Son and shows him all that he himself is doing" (John 5:19,20). In his desert-prayer, Jesus glimpses the divine imperatives that will guide him in the days ahead. In these mountains he clarifies his personal mission, and sees what was important, and what was not. Amidst the rocks, Jesus comes to understand his vocation clearly: the experience crystallizes his sense of direction, his very purpose. Here Jesus clarifies

---

2. We don't have a collection of sayings from the Palestinian monks like the collection of Egyptian sayings in Ward, *Sayings of the Desert Fathers*. Our sayings from Euthymius are mined from Cyril of Scythopolis, *Lives of the Monks of Palestine*, here, 11. See also Binns, *Ascetics and Ambassadors*. For a contemporary exploration of the landscape see Shedadeh, *Palestinian Walks*.

his priorities and his over-arching vision, for he emerges from the desert mountains with one burning mission, one thing on his lips: "Jesus came to Galilee, proclaiming the good news of God, and saying, 'The time is fulfilled, and the kingdom of God has come near; repent, and believe in the good news'" (Mark 1:14, 15). It is precisely amidst the desert mountains that Jesus clarifies to himself the key message that he is entrusted to deliver: the coming of the Reign of God into our midst. At the age of thirty and alone among the rocks, for Jesus everything comes into focus and clear perspective. Matthew's Gospel puts it: "From then onwards" (4:17), Jesus began to preach. Like the very landscape, he lays bare his soul to God. As the wind blows over the desert, so the Spirit, who drove him into the wilderness, breezes into his soul and energizes him for what is to come.

THE EARLY CHURCH IN THE DESERT MOUNTAINS

When the Emperor Constantine, in 313, proclaimed religious freedom throughout the Roman empire for Christians, everything changed for the church: the deserts beckoned once more. And when in 380, the Emperor Theodosius declared Christianity to be the state religion throughout the whole of the empire, Christendom was born, and the call of the desert became louder and irresistible. For after the end of the persecutions, nominalism and mediocrity crept into the church, for now it was so easy to be a Christian—in fact, everyone was a Christian—of sorts. But to some it seemed that the standards of discipleship were being watered down, and only a superficial commitment to Christ was needed. Seeking to rediscover a radical Christianity, first tens, then hundreds, then thousands went to the desert. It was a kind of protest movement. Seeking a more challenging discipleship, they created settlements in the deserts of Egypt, Palestine, Syria and Asia Minor. The red martyrdom of shedding blood was over—this was the "white martyrdom" in which Christians sought to die to the self and allow the Risen Christ to live in them. They went into the desert to discover an authentic spirituality: whether living alone as hermits or together in community, these men and women pursued the same aim—to come face-to-face with God.

In the Byzantine period, the Judean wilderness was flooded with monks seeking seclusion. The title of Derwas Chitty's book, echoing a phrase used by Athanasius in his *Life of Anthony*, sums up the phenomenon:

The Desert a City.[3] At the height of the Byzantine period in the sixth century AD, there were seventy monasteries in the Judean desert. Today one can visit seven living monasteries. In the narrow ravine of the Wadi Pharan, in the desert east of Jerusalem, we find the very first Judean monastery, founded in 275 by St Chariton. Today, a sole Russian monk occupies this cave-complex, the silence broken only by the babble of the nearby spring and by birdsong echoing amidst the sheer white cliffs. The Greek Orthodox monastic village of Mar Saba, dating from the fifth century and one of the oldest continually-occupied monasteries in the world, has grown barnacle-like on the cliffs above the Kidron valley. Also near Bethlehem are the hill-top fortress-monasteries of St Theodosius and St Elias. In the depths of the Wadi Qelt a small community resides at St George of Kobiza, while clinging precariously to the precipitous cliffs above Jericho is the Monastery of the Temptation of Christ. Near the Jordan River, five miles north of the Dead Sea, lies the Greek Orthodox monastery of St Gerasimus. There are also ruins to be discovered: clearly signposted on the road from Jerusalem to Jericho, not far from Bethany (Lazaria) that clings to the eastern flank of the Mount of Olives, we can find amidst the settlement of Ma'ale Adummin[4] the substantial excavated ruins of the monastery of Euthymius.

The First Monks of the Judean Mountains

CHARITON (d.350) founded the first monastery in the Judean desert mountains. An anonymous *Life of Chariton*, written in the sixth century, gives us biographical details and his closing words, which, says the author, were handed down faithfully by his disciples to succeeding generations of monks.

Born towards the end of the third century in Iconium (Konya), as a young man he suffered vicious anti-Christian persecution, but after the Edict of Constantine was able to come to the Holy Land as a pilgrim. Abducted by bandits and brought to a cave in the Pharan Valley, beyond Jeremiah's Anathoth, the *Vita* tells us that after his abductors died by drinking wine poisoned by a snake, Chariton decided to remain a hermit in the cave. There he built a church and pioneered the ascetic lifestyle, establishing a monastery, in Palestine the first ever *lavra*—literally, a lane or alley—shared pathways connecting a cluster of cells. Chariton advised his brothers: "stay

---

3. Chitty, *The Desert A City*. See also Lane, *Solace of Fierce Landscapes*.

4. The name means "Bloody Ascent" referring to the hue of the exposed red limestone rocks, tinted by iron oxide.

calmly in our cells, as in a beehive, and produce the sweet honey of virtue in the manner of bees."[5]

Later he established the lavra of Douka on the ruins of a Hasmonean/Herodian fortress, near the Mount of Temptation above Jericho. After that he moved on to establish a third monastery in Wadi Khureitun, named the Souka or Old Lavra. His biographer tells us: "Wherever he was, Chariton set great value on never being diverted from his life of seclusion . . . Therefore, when he discovered downstream a cave opening in a steep hillside, not far from the this chaste Lavra (what is called to the present day 'St Chariton's hanging place', as it is impossible to climb there, except with a ladder), he thought to take his abode high up there." [6]

As we shall see in the life of Euthymius, the magnetic quality of the spiritual life of these first Christian ascetics and the wisdom they shared in a ministry of spiritual direction, attracted many seekers, and necessitated their relocation in search of solitude. In all three locations his widening fame encouraged Christians to flock to learn from him, disturbing his solitude, which was the reason for him repeatedly moving on.

Chariton's final exhortation to his disciples in the year 350, as mediated to us by the *Vita* is poignant, moving and brimming with desert wisdom.

> In this world are the struggles of the contest, in the other the crowns for those who "compete according to the rules" [2 Tim 2:5, 1 Cor 9: 24- 27]; here belongs the war against the invisible enemies, there the proclamation of the valor; here the pains and the toils, there the prizes and the glory . . . in a word, here is achieved the doing of both good and evil, there the retribution of each . . .
>
> First of all, keep the faith in God steadfast and unshaken in your hearts in every possible way, without ever changing it in whatever peril you may find yourselves . . .
>
> Secondly, pursue peace and the beatitude correlated to it in such a way that, whenever it should happen that you are carried away by the devil's banditry and become angry, "the sun will not go down on your anger," as the apostle says. Indeed, cure the pain of the wrong with repentance and remove from your souls the bearing of malice, a passion hateful to the Lord, in order that "the peace of God, which passes all understanding, will guard your hearts."

---

5. di Segni, "Life of Chariton," 408.

6. di Segni, "Life of Chariton", 411. This monastery has been excavated by Hirschfeld, *Judean Desert Monasteries.*

Flee from avarice, as being the mother of idolatry; love poverty with all your might, so that, in the pursuit of it, you will not fail to become poor in spirit, and to gain the beatitude that comes from this state . . .

Practice your virtues in a hidden corner—either self-discipline, or almsgiving, or earnest prayer accompanied by tears, or collectively speaking, any other good quality of yours—and wait to receive in public the reward for your achievements from "your Father who sees in secret."

Wash the feet of the holy ones who come to visit you . . . You for your part must show pity, in order that you may come out to meet the Bridegroom with the lamps of the soul brightly lit, as the oil naturally makes them glow with radiant light . . .

The purity of the soul is like a splendid garment; for as the garment, being resistant to spoiling, may be brought back to its former cleanliness at any time by being washed whenever it has become soiled, so the soul, originally woven without any taint by God her maker—for she is made in his image and likeness—is at last dirtied by sin, as though by smoke, and her natural beauty becomes dim; but whenever a man's soul is wiped clean by his compassion for the needy and by other worthy fruits of repentance, she regains her former bloom, and then she will rightly be granted to take part in the enjoyment of eternal delights, together with all the guests in the wedding hall, for now the soul will be clad in the whiteness of good deeds and wrapped in a mantle worthy of the Bridegroom . . .

This is said about charity; and what about endurance? Until the last day of your departure, O my children, dare not hope that you will not meet with various trials, for it is written: "My son, if you enter in the service of God, prepare your soul for trial." But do not lose heart, for "God is faithful," says the most wise Paul, "and he will not let you be tempted beyond your strength . . ." Therefore, "you have need of endurance, so that you may do the will of God and receive what is promised." [7]

BASIL THE GREAT (330–379) as he came to be known, discovered authentic Christian discipleship and an astonishing closeness to God in the desert mountains of Judea. He came soon after the death of Chariton and was one of the first to visit the Judean mountains to see for himself what was going on in this counter-cultural monastic experiment. His experience here in 357 was destined to be seminal and transformative. Later he wrote of this

---

7. di Segni, "Life of Chariton," 412.

exploratory time researching monastic life in Palestine.[8] Basil himself tells us the story:

> I have spent many a year in the pursuit of nothingness and I have consumed almost all of my youth in the vain attempt to acquire the teachings of a wisdom which is folly in God's eyes. And then, one day, as waking up from a deep slumber, I looked toward the wonderful light of the truth of the Gospel, and I saw the uselessness of the wisdom of the "rulers of this age, who are doomed to pass away" [1 Cor 2:6]. I wept abundantly on my miserable life and prayed that a hand be extended to introduce me into the principles of piety. Among other things I was eager to straighten myself up, so spoiled had I been by my frequentation of frivolous people. Having read the Gospel and having seen that the best starting point toward perfection was to get rid of one's possessions and to share them with poor brethren, to take no care for this life . . . I wished to find one of the brethren choosing this way of life, so that I could cross with him over the stormy seas of life. I found many such men in Palestine . . .
>
> I wondered at their discipline of life, I wondered at their steadfastness in hardships, I was amazed at their constancy in prayers, how they prevailed over sleep, yielding to no bodily exigency, keeping the affections of their soul always lofty and free from bondage, in hunger and thirst, in cold and nakedness, never giving attention to the body, never willing to worry about it. As if they were living out of the flesh, they did show me by their acts what it means to be a foreigner passing through this world and to have our citizenship in heaven. I admired all this and I regarded the life of these men as blessed for they showed by their actions that they were "carrying in the body the death of Jesus" [2 Cor 4:10], and I wished that, as much as was in me, I could emulate them . . . I envied them for their unusual way of living.[9]

He indeed went on to emulate the monks of the Palestinian desert mountains, for on his return to Pontus in Cappadocia, he immediately sought to develop a similar lifestyle to that modelled by the Judean monks, amidst his own steeply-forested mountains.[10] Basil sold his possessions

8. He also visited monastics in Egypt and Syria.

9. Letter 223 written to Eustathios of Sebastea in 375. Barrois, *Fathers Speak*, 39–40. See also Holmes, *Life Pleasing*, 31.

10. Pontus is itself a biblical mountain in so far as it is the location of a Christian community to which Peter's first letter is addressed (1 Peter 1:1) and on the day of Pentecost people from Pontus are named among the pilgrims (Acts 2:9); the early church

and divided them among the poor. With a small group of friends, he retreated into solitude upon the banks of the river Iris, not far from his family estate at Annesi, in the province of Pontus to begin his monastic life. In this solitude, Basil outlined his first monastic rules which were later formulated into 55 Long Rules, and his counsels to his monks which were arranged into 313 Short Rules. The wisdom contained in the *Asceticon* was discovered in the mountains of the Judean desert. His Rule, embodying the insights he gained from the Judean mountains, not only became the central formative document in eastern monasticism but also shaped western monasticism, as Benedict acknowledges at the conclusion of his own Rule.[11]

Already, within a year of leaving the Judean wilderness, in 358, Basil was writing to his friend Gregory Nazianzus, to persuade him to come and join the retreat at Pontus. This letter enables us to hear Basil's voice as he sketches ideas that will become central in his Rule, exploring four aspects of the call of the desert mountains:

> One should aspire at keeping the mind in quietude. The eye that wanders continually around, now sideways, now up and down, is unable to see distinctly what lies under it; it ought rather to apply itself firmly to the visible object if it aims at a clear vision. Likewise, the spirit of man, if it is dragged about by the world's thousand cares, has no way to attain a clear vision of the truth . . . Each day arrives, each in its own way obscuring the mind; and the nights, taking over the cares of the day, deceive the soul with obnoxious phantasms. There is only one escape: withdraw from the world altogether. Now this withdrawal does not mean that we should leave the world bodily, but rather break loose from the ties of "sympathy" of the soul with the body. This means to be without a city, without a house, without anything of our own, without property, without possessions, without resources, without affairs, without contacts, without being taught by men, but making ready to receive in our heart the imprint of divine teaching . . . The solitude offers a very great advantage for our task . . . Let therefore the site of the monastery be most like our place here [Annesi], free from the commerce of men, so that nothing may come from without and break the continuity of the "askesis", for a pious "askesis"

---

leader Aquila hailed from here (Acts 18:2), and here Evagrius learnt much from Basil, who ordained him a lector.

11. Fry, *Rule of St Benedict*, chapter 73. Basil's teachings on monasticism, as encoded in works such as his *Small Ascetikon*, was transmitted to the West via Rufinus in the 4th century (see chapter 8).

nurtures the soul with divine thoughts. Is there a greater happiness than to imitate on earth the choir of angels? At daybreak, to get up at once for prayer and honor the Creator with hymns and canticles? Then, when the sun shines with its pure light, to rush to work, to be accompanied everywhere with prayer and, so to speak, to season our labor with the salt of hymns; to establish the soul in joy and drive out sadness is the gift and the comfort of the hymns. Quietude is therefore the principle of purification of the soul, when the tongue does not speak the words of men, when the eyes do not turn all around to behold the complexion and the proportion of bodies, when the hearing does not loosen the spirit with sweet tunes composed for pleasure, or with jokes or buffoon cries most apt to unnerve the strength of the soul . . .

The high road leading to the discovery of duty is the study of the inspired Scriptures. In them are found rules of action, and the lives of the blessed which the Scriptures have transmitted to us are like living images of the godly life set before us that we may imitate their good works . . .

Prayers succeeding to lecture rejuvenate and invigorate the soul, which is moved toward God by desire, for beautiful is the prayer that impresses into the mind a clear notion of God. This is properly the "inhabitation" of God, to have God seated in oneself through memory. Thus we become a temple of God, when earthly cares do not interrupt the continuity of memory, when the mind is not disturbed by unforeseen passions and when, fleeing from all things, the friend of God withdraws unto God, drives out all incitements to evil, and holds fast to those practices that lead to virtue.[12]

Basil's voice lays four invitations before us.

First, the desert mountains call us to stillness and silence. Basil writes: "One should aspire at keeping the mind in quietude [*hesychia*] . . ."

Secondly, the desert mountains call us to solitude. Basil explains: "The solitude [*eremia*] offers a very great advantage for our task of prayer. Let us for a season be free from the commerce of men, so that nothing may come from without and break the continuity of the *ascesis*" [training or discipline]. There is a place in discipleship for getting off the treadmill of work and activity, saying goodbye to the clamor of things in the world forever competing for our attention, in order that, for a while at least, we may become focused on God and utterly attentive to him.

---

12. Letter 2 written to Gregory of Nazianzus. Barrios, *Fathers Speak*, 47–49.

Thirdly, the desert mountains call us to detachment. Basil writes: "Now this withdrawal [*anachoresis*, retreat] does not mean that we should leave the world bodily, but rather break loose from the ties of 'sympathy' of the soul with the body." Basil is extolling the virtues of making a retreat from activity, for a few minutes, or hours, or days. He says that, for a season, we have to cut our ties, loosen our grip and grasp on activities, let go of our attachments and of our worries. This is so we can become wholly available to God in prayer.

Fourthly, the desert mountains call us to receptivity. The most important thing, says Basil, is that we are "making ready to receive in our heart the imprint of divine teaching . . . beautiful is the prayer that impresses into the mind a clear notion of God." For Basil and the Desert Fathers and Mothers[13], the overriding aim is learning to listen out for the whisper of God's voice and to discern his will and guidance.

EUTHYMIUS THE GREAT (377–473) led the second generation of monks in the Judean mountains. We learn about him through *The Life of Euthymius* composed by Cyril of Scythopolis. Born in Melitene in Armenia, after ordination he was placed in charge of local monasteries around the city, but he craved solitude and found this responsibility too dissipating and distracting. At the age of 29 he came to the Holy Land as a pilgrim in search of solitude. After venerating the holy places of Jerusalem, he proceeded directly to the desert mountains and "visited the inspired fathers in the desert, studying the virtue and way of life of each one and impressing it upon his own soul."[14] He settled at Chariton's lavra at Pharan, in the Wadi Qelt. Cyril tells us: "In his love of solitude he stayed in a hermit's cell outside the lavra, possessing absolutely nothing of the goods of this age . . . Freeing himself from every earthly care he had as his one sole aim how to please God through prayer and fasting." [15]

Cyril's account often uses the key word *hesychia* (quietude) or *hesychist* (solitary) and tells us of Euthymius' desire to be to be "sundered from all human intercourse and yearning to consort with God in solitude through prayer."[16] After five years, at the age of thirty four, he moved with

---

13. Recently, attention has been directed to the Desert Mothers, an area of current research. See for example, Swan, *Forgotten Desert Mothers*.

14. Cyril, *Lives*, 9.

15. Cyril, *Lives*, 9.

16. Cyril, *Lives*, 10.

his fellow hermit Theoctistus to a cave located on the cliffs of the Wadi Og, as we noted. Later, more hermits joined them to form a *coenobium* (community)—the first in Judean desert. He became famous for healing a son of an Arab leader, and many hermits gathered around him. To remain in solitude, after ten years Euthymius relocated with a fellow hermit Domitian to the mountain ruins of Masada, forming the core of a new lavra. After a time living in the cliff-face caves near Tell-Ziph, southeast of Hebron, where he established a further *coenobium*, he returned to the more remote monastery of Theoctistus because, while he freely offered a ministry of spiritual direction to those who sought him out there, he resolved to safeguard his time alone with God.

Once again, due to his immense popularity, the solitude-seeking hermit moved to a cave west of Theoctistus' monastery on the Adummim hilltop, beside the main road to Jerusalem. In 428 he established here a monastery of hermits based on the model of the lavra of Pharan. This his successor Martyrius developed into a cenobitic community. Euthymius' lasting legacy was to establish the pattern for Palestinian monasticism by insisting that those who desired the eremitical (solitary) life must first be trained in the cenobitic community. His voice echoes across the centuries, calling us to vigilance and alertness and humility:

> Brethren, strive for what brought you out here, and do not neglect your own salvation. You must at all times stay sober and awake. As Scripture says, "Keep awake, and pray not to enter into temptation." Above all recognize this: those who renounce this life must not have a wish of their own but in first place acquire humility and obedience.

Euthymius' experience amongst the mountains reveals 3 paradoxes:

1 Solitude and Hospitality

Though Euthymius sought out his mountain-top as a place of retreat from the world, he was ready to welcome seekers and enquirers with their request for guidance: "Give me a word, Father." His life of prayer was situated within the tension of withdrawal and engagement:

> My child, he who sows with blessings will also reap with blessings. Let us "not neglect to show hospitality, for thereby (as the Apostle says) some have entertained angels unawares" (Heb 13:2).

> Be confident that if you and those after you receive with faith and treat worthily all the strangers and brethren who visit you, the Lord will never fail this place from now on till eternity. For God is well-pleased with such an offering . . . [17]

2 Stability and Movement

Although Euthymius found it necessary to travel from time to time, in search of greater solitude, he is an advocate of stability, of staying put:

> Everywhere we need protection by God's help, wherever we are . . . We ought not to admit evil thoughts that insinuate into us a feeling of resentment or loathing towards the place where we are and towards our companions, or implant accidie [listlessness] or suggest moving to other places, but we must at all times be on our guard and oppose the mind to the wiles of the demons for fear that our rule may be subverted by change of place. For just as a plant that is continuously rebedded cannot bear fruit, so a monk does not bear fruit if he moves from place to place. So if someone resolves to do some good in the place where he is, and is not able to, he should not suppose that he could accomplish it elsewhere. For it is not the place that is in question but the character of the intention.[18]

3 Work and Rest

The first monks were encouraged not only to keep small vegetable gardens but also to engage in crafts like basket-weaving (using the palms and reeds nearby) so they had to live within the dialectic of maintaining deep inner stillness and outward activity:

> In addition to keeping watch on the thoughts within, monks, especially young ones, ought to practice bodily labor, remembering the words of the Apostle, "We labor day and night so as not to be a burden on anyone", and "These hands ministered to me and to those with me." While those in the world endure labor and hardship in order to support wives and children from their work, pay the first-fruits to God, do good according to their power and in addition be charged taxes—it is absurd if we are not even to meet

17. Cyril, *Lives*, 23.
18. Cyril, *Lives*, 26.

the needs of the body from manual labor but to stay idle and immobile, reaping the fruit of the toil of others, especially when the Apostle orders the idle not even to eat.

Cyril adds: "This was the teaching with which our father Euthymius enlightened the community."[19] Euthymius' Final Testament, given in 473, encapsulates his philosophy:

> In all things aim at pure love, the source and goal of every good work and the "bread of perfection." Just as it is not done to eat bread without salt, so it is impossible to achieve virtue without love. For each virtue is made secure through love and humility, with the aid of experience, time, and grace. While humility exalts to a height, love prevents falling from this height, "since he who humbles himself will be exalted" and "love never fails." Love is greater than humility, for it was on account of love for us that God the Word humbled himself to become like us. Therefore we ought to confess him from our hearts and address him with hymns and thanksgivings without ceasing, specially we ourselves who are separate from the manifold affairs of this life, not only because of our pledges to him but also by reason of the undistracted life we lead, freed as we are from the confusion of the world. Therefore let us make every effort to offer up to him purity of soul, chastity of body, and pure love.[20]

Modern writers point out that at the heart of the experience of the Desert Fathers was the quest for inner and outer transformation. Thomas Merton puts it:

> What the Fathers sought most of all was their own true self, in Christ. And in order to do this, they had to reject completely the false, formal self, fabricated under social compulsion in "the world." A life of work and prayer enabled the old superficial self to be purged away and permitted the gradual emergence of the true, secret self in which the Believer and Christ were "one spirit."[21]

Henri Nouwen echoes this view:

> Solitude is not a private therapeutic place. Rather, it is the place of conversion, the place where the old self dies and the new self is born . . . Solitude is the place where Christ remodels us in his own

19. Cyril, *Lives*, 13.
20. Cyril, *Lives*, 54, 55.
21. Merton, *Wisdom of the Desert*, 4, 7.

image and frees us from the victimizing compulsions of the world. Solitude is the place of our salvation.[22]

QUESTIONS FOR TODAY

In a time of a pandemic and its aftermath, we might be tempted to make intercession the focus of our prayers, bringing situations of crisis and need before God. But what if we learnt from the desert mountains, and without setting aside supplication, took another look at the character of our prayers, maybe learning to *listen* to God before we speak? The physical desert, so vital to Jesus and the early church, poses four crucial questions to us today.

1 Dare you open up a space for God in your life?

The Judean mountains are a place of exposure to sun and wind, where there is no hiding place. They call us to seek a spiritual state in which we become naked before God, exposing heart and mind to the wind of his Spirit and the warmth of his love. The desert is a place of persistent erosion, where wind and even water wear down the resistance of stubborn rocks and refashion their shapes. There are unremitting processes of disintegration at work in the desert landscape, as well as processes of formation and building up. So too, in prayer we must learn to become susceptible to God and open to his ever-creative remolding. In prayer, our normal guards need to melt away so that God is allowed to reshape our life and our priorities. As there is an immediacy in the desert, where all props are gone and only essential things matter, so in prayer masks drop off. In prayer we risk facing up in utter honesty to the realities of our lives. From his fourth-century monastery at Bethlehem, Jerome put it: "The desert loves to strip bare."

2 Dare you thirst for more of God in prayer?

The desert mountains speak powerfully of our spiritual poverty. They remind us to confront the aridity of our lives, and to recognize where there might be signs of emptiness. As Macarius wrote: "We have an insatiable longing for the Spirit, to shine out—the more spiritual gifts we enjoy, the more insatiable is the heavenly desire in our hearts, the more hungry and

---

22. Nouwen, *Way of the Heart*, 27, 32.

thirsty we are for more grace."[23] Thus the desert of prayer becomes a place of deep renewal and experience of the Holy Spirit. Isaiah the prophet sees the desert as a symbol of humanity's need—a natural analogy for our need of God. The desert represents spiritual poverty and human thirst for the Divine:

> For I will pour water on the thirsty land,
> And streams on the dry ground.
> I will pour my Spirit upon your descendants,
> And my blessing on your offspring (Isa 44:3; cf. 35:1–10).

3 Dare you embrace prayer itself as pilgrimage and exploration?

We have seen how the desert was a place of pilgrimage and discovery. This invites us to consider the experience of prayer itself as a terrain to be explored, a place of mystery in which we can find out new things about ourselves and about God. Prayer is a quest or search in the holy space which spans ultimacy and intimacy, the discovery of God as Source and as *Abba*. Silences can open up for us desert-like spaces where we find ourselves to be learners of God. The desert rouses us to explore more deeply the mystery of God and the mystery of our self. It attests that we are called to be explorers of the inner space.

4 Whose feet will you wash?

Recalling the event of John 12, Chariton commands his brothers: "Wash the feet of the holy ones who come to visit you." He is emphatic that prayer is not for self-edification but spills over into compassionate action. Euthymius, as we have seen, echoes this conviction, while Basil directly asks those who detach solitude from service: "whose feet will you wash?"[24] Basil's own life on his return from the Judean mountains reveals a dialectic or movement between the poles of solitude and active engagement, between the desert (Pontus) and the city (Caesarea). His Rules are emphatic about the need for monasteries to be outward-looking in compassion to the needs

---

23. Maloney, *Intoxicated with God*, 33.
24. "Longer Rule 7" in Holmes, *Life Pleasing*, 139.

of the community, themselves serving as hospitals and centers of care for the poor.[25]

Our present desert

The four challenges from the desert mountains have particular poignancy in time of pandemic, when we have had to face enforced and imposed lockdowns, not freely-chosen aloneness. The burden of loneliness has been heavy for many, and the challenge has been to convert self-isolation into communion, and loneliness into God-filled solitude. Alone, we have had to face up to our own intensified foibles, but some have had the time and space to rest in God. Viewing this through the lens of the desert helps us to accept such a time as an opportunity to discover ourselves—and God—afresh. Jesus himself experienced the desert to be, at precisely the same time, both testing time and a season of grace, at once trial and formation. The scriptures and the voices of the desert fathers and mothers testify that God does his greatest work in the desert, and we can learn in the desert-time of prayer things we could never have discovered in ordinary, normal circumstances.

FOR PERSONAL REFLECTION

1. What is your experience of solitude? In what ways can you identify with Chariton and Euthymius in their craving for stillness? Basil speaks too of the need for quietude, focus and single-mindedness "to attain a clear vision of the truth." How do you disengage from the pressures of the day when you enter prayer? How do you deal with distractions in prayer?
2. How can we learn from Basil and Euthymius and turn self-isolation into communion, loneliness into solitude? Has the experience of lockdown helped you or hindered you in this respect? How has the experience of social distancing or quarantining challenged you personally?
3. What echoes of Euthymius' paradoxes find in your lifestyle?
4. In what ways do the spiritual journey and quest of Basil resonate with your own?

25. See, for example, "Letter 150", Holmes, *Life Pleasing*.

5. Basil says "break free from the ties of 'sympathy' of the soul with the body." Is this distinction between soul and body helpful—or does such a dualism undermine a more holistic approach to life? Are there "ties of sympathy" that we need to break free from? What place is there for renunciation in today's discipleship?

6. As you explore the mountainous terrain of the desert, how far do you find that physical landscapes mirror the interior life of the human spirit?

6

Galilean Mountains
Inspiring a Unifying Vision

> How beautiful upon the mountains
>   are the feet of the messenger who announces peace,
> who brings good news,
>   who announces salvation (Isa 52:7)

IN THIS STAGE OF our journey we are invited to ascend the Mount of Teaching, the Mount of Healing and the Mount of Commission, and then we will cross the lake to see what mountains are found beyond.

The unpredictable waters of the Sea of Galilee, lying in the deep Jordan rift valley, are bounded on three sides by mountains. The sun rises over the eastern hills of the Golan Heights, down whose steep cliffs ran the Gadarene swine: this is the "Other Side" of the Gospels. Opposite, the town of Tiberias clings precariously to the western cliffs; nearby are the Arbel cliffs, honeycombed by caves in which hid the Jewish rebels of the 130s Bar Kochba Revolt, and the moody hills of the Horns of Hattin where the Crusaders met their fate at the hands of Saladin in 1187. To the north stretch the green, often-forested highlands of Upper Galilee, peppered here and there with Crusader forts. These stretch up to the mountains of Lebanon and, north east, to the snow-capped Mount Hermon, ten thousand feet above sea level, looming above Caesarea Philippi, its meltwaters the source of the Jordan. Evoking its steeply-sided peaks shrouded in cloud, the Bible celebrates the cascading dew of Mount Hermon (Ps 133:3) and suggests it might be a dangerous place, with its "dens of lions... mountains of leopards" (Song 4:8).

Lapped by the waters of Galilee are a series of hills that feature so strongly in the Gospels. Perhaps the best guide to these mountains is St Matthew's Gospel. He mentions three in the range.[1] First the Mount of Teaching, the setting for the Sermon on Mount (ch. 5–7), now known as the Mount of Beatitudes: "When Jesus saw the crowds, he went up the mountain; and after he sat down, his disciples came to him. Then he began to speak, and taught them..." (5:1,2). The second mount is that of healing and feeding:

> Jesus passed along the Sea of Galilee, and he went up the mountain, where he sat down. Great crowds came to him, bringing with them the lame, the maimed, the blind, the mute, and many others. They put them at his feet, and he cured them, so that the crowd was amazed when they saw the mute speaking, the maimed whole, the lame walking, and the blind seeing. And they praised the God of Israel. Then Jesus called his disciples to him and said, "I have compassion for the crowd, because they have been with me now for three days and have nothing to eat; and I do not want to send them away hungry, for they might faint on the way..." (Matt 15: 29–32. The feeding of the 4000 follows).

The whole of the Matthew's Gospel moves towards the climactic moment on the mount of the Great Commission: "Now the eleven disciples went to Galilee, to the mountain to which Jesus had directed them" (28:16).

In his important study *Jesus on the Mountain* Terence Donaldson claims that the six mountains[2] mentioned by Matthew are not only a literacy device, bringing structure to the gospel, but a significant theological symbol, with strong echoes from the Old Testament, appreciated by his Jewish Christian readership. He observes that whenever Jesus is on a mountain there is a resonance with both Mount Sinai and Mount Zion. There is a looking back to the protological mountain of Sinai, where God appears

---

1. These three mountains are conflated in the pilgrim tradition into one sacred hill. The Church of the Multiplication of the Loaves and the Fishes is at the foot of Mount Beatitudes, which also on its lower slopes has a memorial to the Great Commission.

2. The other mountains are the Mount of Temptation (Matt 4), the Mount of Transfiguration (Matt 17), the mount of eschatological discourse (Matt 24, 25). Donaldson, *Jesus on the Mountain*.

Galilean Mountains

in his theophany and gives the Law and Covenant to Moses—celebrating God's purposes in the past. But there is also a looking forward to God's purposes in the future, gospel mountains resonating with Mount Zion, the last mountain, the eschatological mountain and symbol of the End Time, when all peoples will gather in the New Age of the Kingdom. This study alerts us to what we might discover on the mountains. It affirms that when we tread the gospel mountains in Matthew, we learn deeply about two things—we learn something about Christ, who appears on the crests as a figure of awesome authority, giving us insights into his divine sonship. And we learn something about ourselves, about the vocation and destiny of the church—it is very significant that God's people are always on the mountain with Jesus—an image of the eschatological gathering of the community.

The other gospels tell us that the hills above Galilee are mountains of prayer. Luke's gospel emphasizes the place of prayer in Jesus' ministry and gives us special insight into Jesus' interior life. Luke gives us a clear impression of the rhythm in Jesus' ministry between activity and prayer. Jesus' prayer time on the mountains looks like the seedbed of his teaching and the place of his theological reflection, because the silence is broken by Jesus speaking words of instruction. In Luke 6, Jesus withdraws to the hills and prays through the night after a demanding period in which great crowds gathered for preaching and healing (Luke 6:12). Before Jesus makes the major decision about those he will call to be the core of the new people of God, fulfilling the twelve tribes of Israel, he devotes long hours of prayer, in the darkness of the night: "Now during those days he went out to the mountain to pray; and he spent the night in prayer to God. And when day came, he called his disciples and chose twelve of them, whom he also named apostles . . ." (Luke 6:12, 13) This prayer time leads directly to the great Sermon (6:20ff), suggesting that the Beatitudes and Woes took shape and crystalized during his night of prayer. We see a second example in chapter 9 of the gospel. After another period of intense ministry, a further time of prayer on the mountains becomes the context for learning and questions: "Once when Jesus was praying alone, with only the disciples near him, he asked them, 'Who do the crowds say that I am?'" (9:18). At the foot of Mount Hermon/Tabor, after prayer, Jesus teaches about the suffering Son of Man (9:22). Mark's gospel tells us that at the feeding of the 5000 "After saying farewell to them, he went up on the mountain to pray" (6:46).

In recent years, attempting to pinpoint and locate the inspiration that drives Jesus, scholars have characterized him as a "mystic." In his study of the prayer-life of Jesus, Thomson identifies prayer as a crucial source of inspiration and illumination for his ministry.³ In a more recent study, Bruce Chilton characterizes Jesus as a mystic imparting esoteric teaching: "He had already initiated them [the disciples] into his visionary practice, but now he distilled and systemized his mystical insights . . . into a personal tradition *(kabbalah).*"⁴ Marcus Borg sees Jesus as a "Spirit person," interpreting the long periods of prayer mentioned by Luke (6:12) as Jesus' use of contemplation or meditation.⁵ Borg sees Jesus as a Jewish revolutionary mystic and affirms that his mystical experience is the best explanation for his subversive wisdom and his passion and courage as a social prophet. Borg believes that Jesus' radical convictions spring from his prayer-experience, which was marked by a vivid sense of epiphany and divine disclosure.

Other scholars too point to the prayer life of Jesus in the Galilean hills as being the source and spring of his mission. Geza Vermes, in his *Jesus the Jew*, sees Jesus as a Galilean charismatic holy man and miracle-worker in the tradition of Elijah and Elisha. Tom Wright notes the role of receptive prayer in Jesus' experience, remembering that in the return of the Seventy after their mission, within their debriefing and reflection with Christ, perspectives arising from prayer are shared: "Jesus in prayer had seen a vision . . . [he] had seen, in mystical sight, the heavenly reality which corresponded to the earthly victories won by the seventy." ⁶

So, what is a mystic? Is it someone who has been captivated by what Rudolf Otto called *mysterium tremendum et fascinans,* in his classic *The Idea of the Holy*? Barreau affirms: "mysticism is an existential attitude, a way of living at a greater depth."⁷ Jones states: "the mystic is in touch with an 'object' which is invisible, intangible and inaccessible, beyond sensual contact." ⁸ "The Christians of the future will be mystics, or they will not exist at all" wrote Jesuit theologian Karl Rahner, affirming that mysticism

---

3. Thomson, *The Praying Christ*. For a fuller exploration of this see "Jesus the Hermit" and "Jesus the Mystic" in Mayes, *Another Christ* to which this section is indebted.

4. Chilton, *Rabbi Jesus*,175. For a more cautious approach to the prayer of Jesus see Cullmann, *Prayer in the New Testament*.

5. Borg, *Jesus: A New Vision* as discussed in Powell, *The Jesus Debate*.

6. Wright, *Luke for Everyone,* 125.

7. Barreau, "Preface," 8.

8. Jones, "Mysticism, human and divine," 19.

is "a genuine experience of God emerging from the very heart of our existence."[9]

Evelyn Underhill declares that mysticism "is the direct intuition or experience of God; and a mystic is a person who has, to a greater or lesser degree, such a direct experience—one whose religion and life are centered, not merely on an accepted belief or practice, but on that which one regards as first hand personal knowledge."[10] William Wainwright in his work *Mysticism* notes: "While modern English speakers use 'mystical experience' to refer to a wide variety of preternatural experiences, scholars have tended to restrict the term to 'unitary states.'"[11] Scholars speak of mysticism in terms of an experience of "undifferentiated unity" where there are no distinctions between human and divine, between subject and object: these are transcended in a consciousness of union with God where all is one.

Seeing Differently

In Jesus' experience, his mystical openness to the Father is not only a question of first-hand knowledge of God, but also triggers and enables a new and different way of knowing altogether: a different way of seeing the world. The essential thing about his mystical prayer, it seems, is its ability to encompass and enfold into one, into a unity, the diverse and often competing elements of life. Jesus is a seer in more than one sense.[12] He opens his eyes to view the world, its divisions and possibilities, with insight and longing.

As we have seen, Jesus goes *up into the hills* to pray. There he will glimpse a new perspective on things. Down on the shoreline at Capernaum and the lakeside villages, one can see either one coast of Galilee or another. It is not possible to see both opposite coasts at the same time. One can look west and see the city of Tiberias and the nearby northern shore: mainly Jewish, conservative traditional communities. Or, alternatively, one can look east across the waters of the lake to the other side and glimpse enemy territory, the heathen land of the Decapolis, Hellenistic and gentile lands where lurk demoniacs and unclean pigs! One may set one's eyes on one side or another, and an "either/or" choice is involved.

---

9. Rahner, *Theological Investigations 20*, 149.
10. Underhill, *Mystics of the Church*, 9.
11. Quoted in Alston, *Perceiving God*, 25.
12. Witherington, *Jesus the Seer*.

But when you climb up into the hills you see things differently. The higher you climb, the more you see: physically and mystically. You see vistas and panoramas that are able to encompass, in one single view, both sides. You can see both the safe traditional towns that Peter and the disciples dwelt in, and you can see the steep looming cliffs of the Golan Heights to the east—the other side. In his experience of prayer on these very hills, Jesus glimpses a new reality. The lake does not divide, after all—it unites! Both sides, both peoples, both cultures are within the Father's embrace. It is not a question of dualistic "either/or" thinking. It is "both/and." He wants to enfold into his Kingdom all sorts and conditions of people. He longs to criss-cross the lake repeatedly: there is space in the Kingdom for all. Jesus develops a vision for wholeness—for the healing of divides.

James Dunn puts it, we should note "the degree to which Jesus provided a model to his disciples as a man of prayer . . . To be a disciple of Jesus was to pray as Jesus prayed."[13] In his mountain prayer Christ not only exemplifies a balance between prayer and activity, an ebb and flow of stillness and movement, speaking and silence. He reveals to us the very wellsprings of his preaching and ministry. Before it becomes the Mount of Teaching, it is the mount of prayer—where Jesus first listens attentively to his Father, discerning and clarifying his message, in hillside silences broken only by the blowing of the breeze and by the whisper of the Father's voice.

VOICES FROM THE MOUNTAINS OF GALILEE

EGERIA the Spanish pilgrim whom we met in chapter two, describes in the wonderful diary of her travels in the Holy Land her visit to the foot of the mountain now known as Mount of Beatitudes, in 381:

> Not far from Capernaum are some stone steps where the Lord stood [John 21]. And in the same place by the sea is a grassy field with plenty of hay and many palm trees. By them are seven springs [Tabgha], each flowing strongly. And this is the field where the Lord fed the people with the five loaves and the two fishes. In fact the stone on which the Lord placed the bread has now been made into an altar . . . Past the walls of this church goes the public highway on which the Apostle Matthew had his place of custom . . .

---

13. Dunn, *Jesus Remembered*, 561.

Galilean Mountains

> Near there on a mountain is the cave to which the Savior climbed and spoke the Beatitudes.[14]

At the foot of the mountain to which Egeria refers, the Church of the Sermon on the Mount was built in the fourth century. This was destroyed in the seventh century and it was not until 1938 that a new church was built, sited on the summit of the mountain. This octagonal structure, crowned with a dome, reflects the eight Beatitudes, and is looked after by the Franciscan Sisters of the Immaculate Heart of Mary. It is a suitable location to celebrate the Sermon on the Mount for it overlooks a vast natural amphitheater above the Sea of Galilee where one can imagine crowds gathering to listen.

JEROME (342–420) is our main guide to these sacred mountains. A contemporary of Egeria, from 384 he was based in Bethlehem where he translated the old and new testaments into Latin (*Vulgate*). In winter 385 Jerome led a pilgrimage to Galilee and other places for his friend Paula and her daughter Eustochium.[15] In the thirty-four years in which Jerome resided in the Holy Land he no doubt revisited Galilee several times—he certainly made several visits to the north, to use the famed library at Caesarea Maritima. His Latin translation of the guide to place-names *The Onomasticon* of Eusebius, included many fresh details, indicating familiarity with the holy sites throughout the land.[16] As a biblical scholar, Jerome discovered how knowledge of the sites could enhance understanding of the scriptures. He wrote: "In the same way that those who have seen Athens understand the Greek histories better . . . so he who has contemplated Judaea with his own eyes and knows the sites of the ancient cities, and knows the names of the places whether the same or changed, will regard Scripture more lucidly."[17] So let us listen to his voice speaking to us across the centuries, as he reflects on the

---

14. Wilkinson, *Egeria's Travels*, 196.

15. The itinerary is described in the obituary letter (Letter 108) which Jerome wrote to Eustochium in 404 after Paula's death. See Wilkinson, *Pilgrims*, 45–52. Houtman considers Letter 46 "the classical expression of Jerome's positive principal attitude concerning pilgrimage and visits to the holy sites of the Holy Land." Pilgrimage is described as both an emotional experience and a means for a deeper understanding of the Scriptures. Newman, "Jerome and the holy places of Palestine", 220.

16. The *Onomasticon* is a work *On the Place-Names in the Holy Scripture*, a gazetteer giving us knowledge of early fourth century Palestine.

17. From his introduction to the Book of Chronicles. Migne, *Patrologia Latina* 29, 423.

meaning of the mountains of Galilee in his *Commentary on St Matthew's Gospel* written in 398. We follow him as he climbs the three mountains of Galilee: the Mount of Teaching, the Mount of Healing and the Mount of Commission, and then we will cross the lake to listen to what he says about the mountains beyond.

THE MOUNT OF TEACHING—MOUNT BEATITUDES

> *And seeing the crowds, he went up on a mountain, and when he had sat down, his disciples came to him (5:1)*

The Lord goes up to the mountains to draw the crowds toward deeper matters with himself, but the crowds are not capable of ascending. The disciples follow and he speaks to them, not standing, but sitting and drawn in. For they were unable to understand him shining in his majesty . . . From what precedes and what follows, the location is shown to be in Galilee . . . After all, after he finished his words, it immediately follows: "Now when he had entered Capernaum."

> *"Blessed are the poor in spirit" (5:3)*

This is what we read elsewhere: "And he will save the humble in spirit." [Ps 34:18] But lest anyone think that the Lord is preaching that kind of poverty that is sometimes borne by necessity, he has added "in spirit", that you might understand humility, not indigence. "Blessed are the poor in spirit", who on account of the Holy Spirit are poor voluntarily . . .

> *"Blessed are the meek, for they shall possess the land" (5:4)*

He does not mean the land of Judea or the land of this world . . . Rather, he means the land that the Psalmist declares: "I believe that I shall see the good things of the Lord in the land of the living." [Ps 27:13] One who possesses land in this way and who triumphs after the victory is further described in the forty-fourth Psalm: "Set out and proceed prosperously, and reign because of truth and meekness and justice". . .

> *"Blessed are those who mourn, for they shall be consoled" (5:5)*

The mourning recorded here is not the mourning of those who have died in accordance with the common law of nature, but the mourning over those who have died in their sins and vices . . .

"Blessed are those who hunger and thirst for justice" (5:6)

It does not suffice for us to want justice, if we do not experience a hunger for justice. Thus from this example we should understand that we are never sufficiently just, but that it is always necessary to hunger for works of justice.

"Blessed are the merciful" (5:7)

Mercy is understood not only in almsgiving but in [responding to] every sin of a brother. For we are to carry the burdens of one another. [Gal 6:2]

"Blessed are the pure in heart, for they shall see God" (5:8)

He is not referring to those who have no consciousness of sin. A pure man is conspicuous for his pure heart; the temple of God cannot be polluted. [1 Cor 3:16–17]

"Blessed are peacemakers" (5:9)

This refers to those who make peace, first in their own heart, then among dissenting brothers and sisters. For what use is it when others are pacified through you, if within your own heart there are wars of vices going on?

"Blessed are those who suffer persecution for the sake of justice" (5:10)

He has expressly added: "for the sake of justice." For many suffer persecution on account of their sins, and they are not just.[18]

What has Jerome to say about the other Galilean mountains?

THE MOUNT OF HEALING

And going up on the mountain he sat there, and the crowds came to him. And he cured them, so that the crowds were amazed, seeing the mute speaking, the lame walking, the blind seeing; and they praised the God of Israel (15:29–31)

Jesus returns to Judea and to the Sea of Galilee. He goes up a mountain, and, just as a bird challenges its tender fledglings to fly, so he sits down there, and the crowds run to him, leading or carrying with them those who were oppressed by various infirmities

---

18. Jerome, *Commentary*, 74–76.

> . . . Observe that many lame and blind are led to the mountain to be cured by the Lord.[19]

Jerome sees particular significance in the mountain by his allusion to Deuteronomy:

> Just as an eagle stirs up its nest, encouraging its young to fly,
> and then hovers over them in case they need help,
> And spreads its wings and catches them if they fall,
> and carries them up high on its wings
> So the Eternal guided Jacob through the wilderness
> without the help of any foreign god. (Deut 32:11, 12 *Voice* translation)

Jesus had said in the Sermon on the Mount "Look at the birds of the air . . ." (Matt 6:26). The bird can image the conquering of fears and timidity in its fledgling time of quitting the nest and spreading its wings. Jerome evokes the vivid image of a parent eagle rousing chicks in order to get them out of the coziness of the nest. We recall Isaiah's words:

> those who wait for the LORD shall renew their strength,
> they shall mount up with wings like eagles,
> they shall run and not be weary,
> they shall walk and not faint. (Isa 40:31)

The mountain of healing is not only a nest, a place of safety and refuge for the vulnerable, it is also a launching-pad, a springboard, for mission. Our experience of Christ's healing, his salve upon our woundedness, leads us to action and to ministry, for immediately "Jesus asked them, 'How many loaves have you?' . . . the disciples gave them to the crowds" (15:34,36). This is an echo of the feeding of the 5000 where Jesus, after healing the people, commands his disciples "*You* give them something to eat" (14:16). This empowering for ministry is brought to a crescendo in the third Galilean mountain.

THE MOUNT OF THE GREAT COMMISSION

Not once but three times[20] Matthew's gospel tells us that the Risen Christ will see his disciples not in the religious center of Jerusalem, the place of the

---

19. Jerome, *Commentary*, 184.

20. Jesus in Gethsemane (26:32) and at the tomb (28:10); the angels at the tomb (28:7).

Galilean Mountains

religious establishment, but in the marginal land of Galilee. Jerome points to its significance:

> *Go announce to my brethren that they should go to Galilee. They will see me there (28:10)*

> It is not in Judea that they will see the Savior, but in the multitude of the Gentiles.

Jerome alludes to the phrase "Galilee of the Gentiles" (Isa 9:1) which literally means "circle of pagans." Much more mixed in terms of Jewish and Gentile populations than other regions of the land, the Galilee was a semi-autonomous frontier region, exposed to the nearby foreign countries and ethnicities. Studies by Horsley and Freyne illuminate for us the marginality of Galilee.[21] Freyne calls Galilee "a symbol of the periphery becoming the new non-localized center of divine presence."[22] It maintained both a physical distance from the Temple on Zion and an ideological distance, prepared to make a critique of the self-serving Jerusalem clerical elite and their practices. It found itself on the edges. Princeton theologian Sang Lee observes:

> Galileans were not just left alone in their liminal situation but were oppressed, dehumanized and looked down upon. Galileans were marginalized by foreign invaders and also by the Jerusalem Temple-state . . . Galilee was repeatedly invaded and exploited by foreign empires throughout its history.[23]

But above all, it was a place of deep poverty and need. The Risen Christ is saying: "Galilee—I will see you *there*. I will meet you in the places that need healing and encouragement. No need to look for me in the corridors of power or at the religious center. I will be found among the poor, the broken and hurting. Find me among the rejected and stigmatized. I wait for you in situations of injustice and dehumanization. *There* I will meet you." And what does Jerome notice about the climax of Matthew's gospel?

> *Now the eleven disciples went to Galilee, to the mountain that Jesus had appointed for them (28:16)*

> After the Resurrection Jesus is seen on a mountain in Galilee, and he is worshiped there, though some doubt, and their doubt increases our faith . . .

21. Freyne, *Jesus, A Jewish Galilean*. Horsley, *Archaeology, History and Society*.
22. Freyne, *Galilee, Jesus and the Gospels*, 54.
23. Lee, *From a Liminal Place*, 47.

> *And Jesus came and spoke to them saying "All authority in heaven and on earth has been given to me" (28:18)*
>
> Authority has been given to him who a little earlier was crucified, who was buried in a tomb, who lay there dead, who afterward was resurrected. But authority has been given "in heaven and on earth." Thus he who was previously reigning in heaven reigns on earth through the faith of believers.
>
> *"Go therefore, teach all nations, baptizing them in the name of the Father, and of the Son, and of the Holy Spirit" (28:19)*
>
> First they teach all nations, then they dip in water those who have been taught. For it is not possible that the body receives the sacrament of Baptism unless the soul first receives the truth of the faith . . .
>
> *"Teaching them to observe all things whatsoever I have commanded you" (28:20)*
>
> The sequence is extraordinary. He has commended the apostles first to teach all nations, then to dip them in the sacrament of faith, and after faith and baptism they are to instruct them in the things that must be observed. And lest we think the things that are commanded are light matters, he added the few words: "all things whatsoever I have commanded you." Thus those who believe, who are baptized in the Trinity, must do everything that has been taught.
>
> *"And behold, I am with you all the days until the consummation of the age" (28:20)*
>
> He promises to be with his disciples until the consummation of the age. He shows that they will always be victorious and that he will never depart from believers . . . [24]

A recurrent theme in Jerome's reflections is the power of faith—through the faith of believers Christ can reign on earth. But this faith, fueled by transformative teaching on the mountains, strengthened by the experience of healing on the summits, is inseparable from obedience and from action. Such a faith, engendered by the mountaintop encounters, will renew the whole world and enable believers to "always be victorious."

---

24. Jerome (Scheck, *Commentary*, 327–28.

THE MOUNTAINS OF THE OTHER SIDE

Have you ever noticed how many times in the gospels Jesus says: "Let us go over to the other side"? For example, Matthew tells us: "Immediately he made the disciples get into the boat and go on ahead to the *other side*, while he dismissed the crowds" (14:22); "When the disciples reached the *other side*, they had forgotten to bring any bread" (16:5). Jesus asks his disciples to quit the security of Capernaum, a safe, conservative, traditional, mainly Jewish town, and to traverse the uncertain waters to risk an entry into enemy territory, pagan, Gentile terrain, Greco-Roman land, shores populated by unclean demoniacs and Gadarene pigs.

The dark basalt hills of the Golan Heights, known in the Bible as the Kingdom of Og of Bashan,[25] which come down as a sharp escarpment to Galilee's eastern shore in the Rift Valley, look bleak and forbidding from a distance, when viewed from the northern side of the Lake, but they turn out to be surprisingly fruitful and fertile. Normally, it is a place to be avoided: to go there would contaminate the devout Jew. But Jesus calls his disciples to quit their safety zone and risk encounter with the Other, with those who are definitely "not us." Even today, the Golan Heights are a no-go military zone!

Significantly, Mark's gospel tells us, that Jesus went directly from his encounter with the Syro-phoenician Woman to the pagan territories of the Decapolis: "Then he returned from the region of Tyre, and went by way of Sidon towards the Sea of Galilee, in the region of the Decapolis" (Mark 7:31). The Greek text says "he went into the midst of the district of the Decapolis." He was empowered and inspired by his meeting with the Other represented in the Syro-phoenician Woman to go straight to areas on the very frontier of the Roman Empire: the group of ten cities marked by Greek culture, nine of which lay beyond the confines of ancient Israel (located in present day Jordan and Syria). Jesus led his disciples here that they might discover the Hellenistic way of life so different to Jewish values. Indeed, Jews were often affronted and dismayed by aspects of this foreign world: by the nude-wrestling, the gymnasia and the theatres. He wanted them to experience culture-shock!

Matthew tells us that later Jesus again crossed over to the eastern region beyond the Jordan, and he locates significant encounters and teaching there. The enemy, pagan terrain becomes the land of salvation, for it is in these foreign parts, for example, according to Matthew's perspective, that

---

25. This features in the narratives of Numbers and Deuteronomy.

he meets the "rich young ruler" (Matt 19:16–22). Indeed, Matthew tells us that Jesus' fame spreads through all Syria and he welcomes folk from the foreign lands of the Decapolis and beyond the Jordan to hear his preaching and experience his healing (Matt 4:23–25).

Matthew specifically mentions the "steep bank" of the mountains of Bashan on the "other side" in his account of the deliverance of the demoniacs at Gadara:

> Now when Jesus saw great crowds around him, he gave orders to go over to the other side . . . When he came to the other side, to the country of the Gadarenes, two demoniacs coming out of the tombs met him. They were so fierce that no one could pass that way . . . the whole herd rushed down the steep bank into the sea and perished in the waters . . . (8:18, 28, 32)

The scary hills of the Other Side, often seen in shadow (because the sun rises beyond them) become a place of healing, a land of liberation. This is Matthew's conviction about the mountains of the Other Side. There are no places which can exclude the light of Christ, even if it's overwhelming, as the villagers discovered, for Jerome reminds us what happened after the exorcism of the demoniacs:

> *Behold, the whole city went out to meet Jesus, and when they saw him they asked him to move on from their borders (8:34)*

> Those who ask him to move on from their borders do this not out of pride (as some think) but out of humility. They judge themselves unworthy of the presence of the Lord, just as Peter did also at the catch of the fish, when he fell down at the knees of the Savior and said "Depart from me, Lord, for I am a sinful man."[26]

QUESTIONS FOR TODAY

Today we see many places on earth riven by division. Elections in the USA have expressed bitter polarities; in the UK Brexit has fractured the nation; in the Holy Land itself Jew and Arab are pitted against one another. There seems to be a natural human tendency towards polarization, keeping things apart. It has to do with being in control, trying to make sense of things neatly, seeing things in black and white, but as we know it

---

26. Jerome (Scheck, *Commentary*, 105.

Galilean Mountains

can lead to fundamentalism, racism, homophobia, fear of the other. We feel safer when we oppose, judge, differentiate, label and compare. Today, we live in a polarized world: republican vs. democrat, conservative vs. labor, protestant vs. catholic, east vs. west. Bifurcation is the preferred option. It has been said, we live in a "tit for tat universe."[27] Computers, which increasingly rule our lives, are based on a binary system. McAfee Brown calls this addiction to duality "the great fallacy."[28] The pandemic has exposed deep disparities between the haves and the have-nots. It has revealed searing inequalities at the local level within our communities, within national society and at the international level between rich and poor countries in the race to obtain vaccines.

The healing of divides and a quest for wholeness and reconciliation have been recurring themes discovered on the Galilean mountains. In pondering the Beatitudes Jerome grapples with oppositions between material poverty and spiritual poverty, between physical territory and spiritual land, between natural mourning and spiritual grief. Reflecting on the call to be peacemakers, he struggles with the twofold need to be reconciled with others while finding reconciliation and peace within the divided self. In his thinking about the mountain of the Great Commission he sees a tension between heaven and earth, and a tension between ritual and life—the rite of baptism must be matched with obedience, ceremonial with commandment.

Such tensions come to a head on the Gadarene slopes of the Other Side. The demoniac sums up in himself and encapsulates the person pulled in different directions: "Then Jesus asked him, 'What is your name?' He replied, 'My name is Legion; for we are many'" (Mark 5:9). He is a tormented and divided soul. His very name suggests that many conflicting forces are battling for his soul. The account in Mark 5 prompts us to face several questions of ourselves:

He lived among the tombs

What things in your life are leading to death?

The chains he wrenched apart

What agitates you or disturbs you? What stresses you? What menaces you? What do you feel constraining or restricting in your life, holding you down? What is there in you that is desperate to get out, to find release or expression? It may be something negative, like anger; it could be something

---

27. Rohr, *Naked Now*, 77.
28. McAfee Brown, *Spirituality and Liberation*.

wholly positive, like unfulfilled creativity, unexpressed emotions, undeveloped talent.

He was always howling

What is your heart's cry right now?

(He was) bruising himself with stones

What causes your integrity or peace of mind hurt or harm? What damages your self-image?

He ran and bowed down before him

We are invited to turn our focus to the radiant and mysterious person of Christ

My name is Legion, for we are many

What are the competing claims in your life? Do they pull you apart, pull you in different directions? Do you feel fragmented?

Send us into the swine

What repressed or suppressed elements in you need to be expressed, released? They need to be breathed out . . .let go of, and passed into God's hands.

Sitting at the feet of Jesus

As we sit at the feet of Jesus, we allow his healing to envelop the soul. There, we can embrace the wholeness he wants to bring us. We realize that we don't have to be perfect. We accept our limitations and remind ourselves that we have a treasured, cherished place in the presence of Jesus. Jesus has accepted us: we can accept ourselves. We contrast the verbs in the early verses of Mark 5: binding, wrenching apart, breaking in pieces, crying out, bruising. Now the guy is *sitting*. Jesus has brought him to a place of stillness, resting in the new reality. We too can practice it. We can let go of the bruising, cutting, wrenching. We can let go, too, of the self-violence of the blaming, the judging, the comparing. We can learn to *sit*, still, at the feet of Jesus.

clothed and in his right mind

The man's dividedness, represented by the "Legion", split him apart. Now he is given a renewed mind. The divided, torn-apart mind has been clothed with "the mind of Christ." Now he is integrated, one, because Jesus has given him a new, unifying focus and mission. To this divided self Jesus brings a radical re-ordering—a fresh center of gravity, a refocused centeredness, a new identity and a healing unity. As we wait in the silence, we can allow Jesus to clarify us a renewed sense of purpose.

> *Go home to your friends*
>
> We allow Christ to give us, again, an over-arching vision of what we are to be, a vision that unifies our fragmentedness. How would you sum up your essential vocation in one word? What is the over-arching vision and purpose, uniting and integrating your life and ministry?
>
> *Tell them how much the Lord has done for you*
>
> We rise from sitting at the feet of Jesus, and take some strides forward into the new future he has opened up for us.

A UNIFYING VISION

The Galilean mountains, above all, testify of Jesus' central, unifying vision: the Kingdom of God, which enfolds all.

The Mount of Teaching gives us Beatitudes bracketed and framed by the Kingdom—the first one and the last one declare its promise—telling us that the Beatitudes are all about life in the Kingdom, life lived under God's sovereignty:

> Blessed are the poor in spirit, for theirs is the kingdom of heaven. (5:3)
>
> Blessed are those who are persecuted for righteousness' sake, for theirs is the kingdom of heaven. (5:10)

This is a vision that heals every dichotomy and divide: "I tell you, many will come from east and west and will eat with Abraham and Isaac and Jacob in the kingdom of heaven" (Matt 8:11).

The Mount of Healing and Feeding fulfils Jesus' mission. As Matthew had written earlier, the unifying vision of the Kingdom is the very heart of Jesus mission: "Jesus went about all the cities and villages, teaching in their synagogues, and proclaiming the good news of the kingdom, and curing every disease and every sickness" (9:35).

On the Mount of Commission, we see the uniting reconciling power of the Kingdom on a cosmic scale. It is to embrace all nations on earth: "So go and make followers of all people in the world." (Matt 28: 19, ERV).

On the mountains of the Other Side we not only see Legion restored into unity, we also see in this location episodes revealing Jesus' longing to enfold even the little, insignificant ones—despite opposition—into the Kingdom. No one is to be excluded:

> Little children were being brought to him in order that he might lay his hands on them and pray. The disciples spoke sternly to those who brought them; but Jesus said, "Let the little children come to me, and do not stop them; for it is to such as these that the kingdom of heaven belongs." And he laid his hands on them and went on his way. (Matt 19:13–15)

In today's fracturing world, how can such a radical vision of the inclusive, reconciling Kingdom of God impact on your life and situation? As New Testament scholar Stephen Need puts it: "It is clear that Jesus did not think of the kingdom of God as lying in the future or in the other world. Nor did he see it as an individual, personal or spiritual thing. He saw the kingdom as God's rule for the whole of creation bringing about a new age in which all people would be included. Jesus' teaching, preaching and healing concerned a physical, tangible this-worldly reality affecting everyone . . . it concerned life as actually lived, communities as they relate to each other and societies as they treat each other."[29] This is the call from the Galilean mountains.

FOR PERSONAL REFLECTION

1. As Donaldson suggests, on the mountains of the gospel we learn about two things: something new about the identity and work of Jesus, and something fresh about our own identity and vocation too. What have you learned from the mountains of Galilee?
2. What do you make of Jerome's interpretation of the Beatitudes? Is there anything you would question—or affirm?
3. "Just as an eagle stirs up its nest, encouraging its young to fly . . ." (Deut 32:11). Reflecting on this image of a parent bird challenging its

---

29. Need, *Following Jesus*, 57

Galilean Mountains

fledglings to fly—in what way, do you think, you are being pushed out of your nest, towards the edge of your comfort zone, and needing to find wings?

4. "The higher you climb, the more you see: physically and mystically." Do you agree with this? What is your experience?

5. What does the "Other Side" represent in your context? Is it beckoning you in some way? How are you responding?

7

Tabor
Transforming Perception

> As I live, says the King,
>   whose name is the Lord of hosts,
> one is coming
>   like Tabor among the mountains,
>   and like Carmel by the sea. (Jer 46:18)

ONE OF THE EARLIEST references to Mount Tabor in the Bible is in the narrative about the striking female leader Deborah (Judges 4). She recognized the strategic importance of the mountain, and makes it a vital stronghold and base in her struggle with Sisera. Indeed, throughout its history Tabor has been a strategic hilltop, overlooking the wide Jezreel valley and commanding fine views of the Via Maris, the ancient route between Egypt and Assyria. At both ends of the valley, military strongholds kept watch from strategic mountains. To the west, Megiddo has from 3000BC up to recent times sought to hold domination over traders and invaders seeking entry into the valley: this is the Biblical *Armageddon*, marked by the fortifications of many successive powers. Mount Moreh broods over the eastern end of the plain: here Gideon assembled his army against the Midianites (Judg 7:1). Adjacent is Mount Gilboa, where Saul and Jonathan perished at the hands of the Philistines (1 Sam 31), and nearby the Romans built a formidable military installation on Beth Shean's high ground, looming over the route from the Jordan Valley. Tabor finds itself half-way along the plain of Jezreel, and Josephus tells us that the Romans established a garrison at its crest, on the site that King Solomon himself had fortified. Both the Muslims and Crusaders built imposing fortresses on the summit of the holy mountain as they sought to command control of the area: a deep defensive ditch encircles the top of Tabor to this day.

But it is pre-eminently a place of beauty and mystery. Mount Tabor rises majestically, an intriguing oval shape, two thousand feet above the Plain. Its thickly-wooded sides, fragrant with pine, seem to point up to heaven itself. It is exposed to the elements, and often shrouded in low mist or cloud. Its transcendent quality accounts for its identification by the Byzantines as the place of the Transfiguration.[1]

In this chapter we explore Mount Tabor as a spiritual borderland, as a place of transition where sky meets soil, where glory and passion mingle. Jesus takes his disciples to a sublimely liminal place, the edge of heaven, the brink of eternity. The gospel reveals that Jesus is motivated by particular intention: he "led them up a high mountain apart" (Matt 17:1, RSV). Decisively, he leads them to a place where the barrier between heaven and earth is breached, where two worlds meet. The barriers of time are dissolved, as Moses and Elijah appear with Jesus, and the past encounters the present, embracing the future. Mortality and immortality interpenetrate in the radiant person of Christ. The Divine reveals itself in the human, and physicality of Christ's body shines with immaterial light. The mountain turns out to be a place of breakthrough, a watershed in the gospel accounts, a pivotal moment, pointing to another mountain, Calvary. Tabor is a "thin place" where the veils which separate are ripped apart. It is an unpredictable place. One minute the disciples are incandescent with divine light and the next they are soaked in a wet fog.

The different gospels bring various emphases to the story. Matthew (17:1–9) heightens the drama: the disciples fall on their faces in fear and awe, and the transcendent Christ—whose face "shone like the sun"—reveals great tenderness as he comes to them, touches them and helps them arise. Here there is the contrast between ultimacy and intimacy. Mark (9:2–10) describes how "his clothes became dazzling white, such as no one on earth could bleach them." Mark suggests that the theophany of the Transfiguration is about the seeing the Kingdom of God coming with power (9:1–8).

---

1. Some scholars believe that Mount Hermon is the site of the Transfiguration.

Tabor

In his account (9:28–36), Luke gives us Jesus as a model of prayer. We are to learn how to pray from the account of the Transfiguration. Luke tells us that not only did Jesus go up the mount to pray, but the prayer-experience itself became the place of *metamorphosis*—the word we translate as transfiguration. Luke says: "he went up the mountain to pray. And as he was praying . . . the appearance of his face changed" (9:28, 29). What changes might we expect in the experience of prayer?

TRANSFORMATION

The eastern tradition of spirituality celebrates the uncreated light of Tabor—the dazzling healing light of the Transfiguration—as a key theme. The Eastern Church considers that it is the disciples, not Christ, who are changed. Their perception is enlarged, their understanding is transfigured. Lossky explains:

> The Transfiguration was not a phenomenon circumscribed in time and space; Christ underwent no change at that moment, even in his human nature, but a change occurred in the awareness of the apostles, who for a time received the power to see their Master as He was, resplendent in the eternal light of His Godhead. The apostles were taken out of history and given a glimpse of eternal realities . . . To see the divine light with bodily sight, as the disciples saw it on Mount Tabor, we must participate in and be transformed by it, according to our capacity. Mystical experience implies this change in our nature, its transformation by grace.[2]

The change occurs in the disciples to the extent that they allow themselves to become not spectators but participants in the divinity revealed to them. The Transfiguration event is truly a threshold of the Divine as the disciples are caught up into the radiant light of Christ. Dare we enter the divine light—even participate in the energies of God—if it might alter us, reshape us, make us different?

GREGORY PALAMAS (1296–1359) is our guide to the mysteries of Mount Tabor. Though he lived on another holy mountain—Mount Athos in Greece—he long pondered the transformative meaning of the event of Mount Tabor. The light of Tabor infiltrated and illuminated every aspect of his writing. Though in the fourteenth century the Eastern Church affirmed

---

2. Lossky, *Mystical Theology*, 22.

the validity of Palamas' teaching, for the past six hundred years his concepts have been almost forgotten, rediscovered only in the mid-20th century, through the scholarly work of pioneers such as Dumitru Stăniloae, John Meyendorff and others.[3] We begin with a sermon he gave for the feast of the Transfiguration...

> For an explanation of the present Feast and understanding of its truth, it is necessary for us to turn to the very start of today's reading from the Gospel: "Jesus took Peter, James and John his brother, and led them up onto a high mountain by themselves" (Matt 17:1).
>
> What does the preceding turn of speech indicate, where the Savior, in teaching His disciples, said to them: "For the Son of Man shall come with his angels in the glory of His Father," and further: "Amen I say to you, there are some standing here who shall not taste death, until they have seen the Son of Man coming in His Kingdom" (Matt 16:27–28)? That is to say, it is the Light of His own forthcoming Transfiguration which He terms the Glory of His Father and of His Kingdom...
>
> God manifests Himself upon the Mount, on the one hand coming down from His heights, and on the other, raising us up from the depths of abasement, since the Transcendent One takes on mortal nature. Certainly, such a manifest appearance by far transcends the utmost limits of the mind's grasp, as effected by the power of the divine Spirit.
>
> Thus, the Light of the Transfiguration of the Lord is not something that comes to be and then vanishes, nor is it subject to the sensory faculties, although it was contemplated by corporeal eyes for a short while upon a mountaintop. But the initiates of the Mystery, the disciples of the Lord at this time passed beyond mere flesh into spirit through a transformation of their senses, effected within them by the Spirit, and in such a way that they beheld what, and to what extent, the divine Spirit had wrought blessedness in them to behold the Ineffable Light...
>
> "What does it mean to say: He was transfigured?" asks the Golden-Mouthed Theologian (John Chrysostom). He answers this by saying: "It revealed something of His Divinity to them, as much and insofar as they were able to apprehend it, and it showed the indwelling of God within Him." The Evangelist Luke says: "And as He prayed, His countenance was altered" (Luke 9:29); and from the Evangelist Matthew we read: "And His face shone as the sun" (Matt 17:2). This is to show that Christ God, for those living and

---

3. Staniloae, *Experience of God*; Meyendorff, *St.Gregory*.

contemplating by the Spirit, is the same as the sun is for those living in the flesh and contemplating by the senses. Therefore, some other Light for the knowing the Divinity is not necessary for those who are enriched by divine gifts.

That same Inscrutable Light shone and was mysteriously manifest to the Apostles and the foremost of the Prophets at that moment, when the Lord was praying. This shows that what brought forth this blessed sight was prayer, and that the radiance occurred and was manifest by uniting the mind with God, and that it is granted to all who, with constant exercise in efforts of virtue and prayer, strive with their mind towards God. True beauty, essentially, can be contemplated only with a purified mind. To gaze upon its luminance assumes a sort of participation in it, as though some bright ray etches itself upon the face . . .

We believe that at the Transfiguration He manifested not some other sort of light, but only that which was concealed beneath His fleshly exterior. This Light was the Light of the divine nature, and as such, it was uncreated and divine. So also, in the teachings of the Fathers, Jesus Christ was transfigured on the Mount, not taking upon Himself something new nor being changed into something new, nor something which formerly He did not possess. Rather, it was to show His disciples that which He already was, opening their eyes and bringing them from blindness to sight. For do you not see that eyes that can perceive natural things would be blind to this Light?

Thus, this Light is not a light of the senses, and those contemplating it do not simply see with sensual eyes, but rather they are changed by the power of the divine Spirit. They were transformed, and only in this way did they see the transformation taking place amidst the very assumption of our perishability, with the deification through union with the Word of God in place of this . . .

Hence it is clear that the Light of Tabor was a divine Light. And the Evangelist John, inspired by divine revelation, says clearly that the future eternal and enduring city "has no need of the sun or moon to shine upon it. For the Glory of God lights it up, and the Lamb will be its lamp" (Rev 21:23). Is it not clear, that he points out here that this Lamb is Jesus, Who is divinely transfigured now upon Tabor, and the flesh of Whom shines, is the lamp manifesting the Glory of divinity for those ascending the mountain with Him?

John the Theologian also says about the inhabitants of this city: "they will not need light from lamps, nor the light of the sun, for the Lord God will shed light upon them, and night shall be no more" (Rev 22:5). But how, we might ask, is there this other light, in which "there is no change, nor shadow of alteration" (Jas 1:17)? What light is there that is constant and unsetting, unless it be the Light of God? Moreover, could Moses and Elias be shining with any sort of sensory light, and be seen and known? Especially since it was written of them: "they appeared in glory, and spoke of his death, which he was about to fulfill at Jerusalem" (Luke 9:30–31). And how otherwise could the Apostles recognize those whom they had never seen before, unless through the mysterious power of the divine Light, opening their mental eyes?

Let us, considering the Mystery of the Transfiguration of the Lord in accord with their teaching, strive to be illumined by this Light ourselves and encourage in ourselves love and striving towards the Unfading Glory and Beauty, purifying our spiritual eyes of worldly thoughts and refraining from perishable and quickly passing delights and beauty which darken the garb of the soul and lead to the fire of Gehenna and everlasting darkness. Let us be freed from these by the illumination and knowledge of the incorporeal and ever-existing Light of our Savior transfigured on Tabor, in His Glory, and of His Father from all eternity, and His Life-Creating Spirit, Whom are One Radiance, One Godhead, and Glory, and Kingdom, and Power now and ever and unto ages of ages. Amen.[4]

The Transformation of Perception

Gregory delights in the theme of discovery of the Divine on Tabor: it is not so much that Jesus was changed in the event of the Transfiguration, but that the perception of the disciples was enlarged—they learned to see things differently. This echoes Luke's account: "Now Peter and his companions were weighed down with sleep; *but when they were fully awake* they saw his glory" (9:32). This is not only a physical stirring but an awakening of their spiritual senses and an expansion of their capacity to sense the Divine, the gift of a new perception, new alertness, a transformation of their senses, effected within them by the Spirit. Now they can see the unseen, and comprehend the incomprehensible. Gregory can hardly contain his excitement when he says that we all have the potential for such a sensing of the Divine: "This shows that what brought forth this blessed sight was prayer, and that the radiance occurred and was manifest by uniting the mind with God, and

---

4. Palamas, "Homily on the Transfiguration." For another translation see Daley, *Light on the Mountain*.

that it is granted to all who, with constant exercise in efforts of virtue and prayer, strive with their mind towards God."

The mystery of Mount Tabor tells us that there are different ways of seeing. There is natural sensing and also spiritual perception, seeing as it were another dimension that can be easily missed. The event of Mount Tabor is at once an unveiling and divine disclosure and an unleashing and unfettering of human faculties, an unlocking of shuttered inner eyes. Christ permanently reveals his glory; he does not hide it. It is our disbelief and spiritual blindness that limits us and holds us back from perceiving the divine shining of Christ's glory. We are challenged to live with a heightened sense of awareness and alertness to the Divine, which is enabled by a synergy of our longing and the working in us of the Holy Spirit.

Such illumination and enlightenment, bringing the deepest kind of spiritual knowledge comes, teaches Gregory, through *theoria*. Andrew Louth explains:

> The word *theoria* is derived from a verb meaning to look, or to see: for the Greeks, knowing was a kind of seeing, a sort of intellectual seeing. Contemplation is, then, knowledge, knowledge of reality itself, as opposed to knowing how: the kind of know-how involved in getting things done. To this contrast between the active life and contemplation, there corresponds a distinction in our understanding of what it is to be human, between . . . puzzling things out, solving problems, calculating and making decisions . . . and being receptive of truth, beholding, looking—referred to by the Greek words *theoria* or *sophia* (wisdom) or *nous* (intellect) . . . Human intelligence operates at two levels: a basic level concerned with doing things, and another level concerned with simply beholding, contemplating, knowing reality.[5]

Palamas teaches that today we can experience for ourselves a vision of divine radiance that is the same light that was manifested to Jesus' disciples on Mount Tabor at the Transfiguration. Such *theoria* is enabled by the Holy Spirit, first given in baptism and fostered by participation in the sacraments of the church, the performance of works of faith and above all by prayer.

---

5. Louth, "Theology," 64–73.

Human Transfiguration and Deification

Gregory was a main proponent of the prayer of *hesychia* (stillness). He puts it: "In prayer . . . man is called to *participation* in divine life: this participation is also the true knowledge of God."[6] In his controversy with the Calabrian philosopher Barlaam, Palamas is insistent: "But hesychasts know that the purified and illuminated mind, when clearly participating in the grace of God, also beholds other mystical and supernatural visions . . ."[7] His opponent Barlaam had denied such possibility, maintaining that God was unknowable and cannot be experienced in this life. But Gregory crafts an important distinction—already found in the Cappadocian Fathers like Gregory of Nyssa and Basil—between the utter transcendence of God—his essence—and the way God touches and transforms human lives—his uncreated energies. His essence will forever be beyond us, but if we are open, we can experience for ourselves, as did the apostles on Tabor, the very energies of God enlivening us and fueling us.

For Gregory this enables the divinization of humanity, permeated and renewed by the divine energies: "They were transformed, and only in this way did they see the transformation taking place amidst the very assumption of our perishability, with the deification through union with the Word of God in place of this . . ." (from sermon above). This is an echo of Athanasius' dictum: "God became human that humans might become God." Men and women can become godlike, sharing in divine attributes: "he has granted to us his precious and very great promises, that through these you may escape from the corruption that is in the world because of passion, and become partakers of the divine nature." (2 Pet 1:4, RSV). This is an awesome view of the very purpose of human life, our fundamental vocation and destiny. A human life is invited to be a transformative journey as one becomes permeated and infused by the divine energies and we progress towards ever closer union with God and identification with God. Maximos—much admired by Gregory—had written in the seventh century "When the intellect (*nous*) practices contemplation, it advances in spiritual knowledge . . . the intellect is granted the grace of theology when, carried on wings of love . . . it is taken up into God and with the help of the Holy Spirit discerns—as far as this is possible for the human intellect—the

---

6. Meyendorff, *Byzantine Theology*, 77.

7. Palamas, *Triads*, 58. In 1351 Hesychast teaching was confirmed as the doctrine of the Eastern Orthodox Church.

qualities of God."[8] Such knowledge is transforming: "The intellect joined to God for long periods through prayer and love becomes wise, good, powerful, compassionate, merciful and long-suffering; in short, it includes with itself almost all the divine qualities."[9]

In Gregory's view, deification is a return to humanity's original condition. Created in the image of God, humans actualize the likeness through union with God. The fall of Adam meant his separation from beauty and light but in Christ we regain the lost beauty of holiness after the image of God. The vision of the divine light is a return to the innocent state of humanity: in paradise, Adam was clothed with a garment of light, which he lost through sin; on Tabor, Christ clothes the disciples with this shining garment.

Tabor—Today!

Gregory believes that the experience and promise of Mount Tabor does not belong only to past history or to a future hope of divine light in heaven. It is for today, for us to discover right now:

> The transformation of our human nature, its deification and transfiguration—were these not accomplished in Christ from the start, from the moment He assumed our nature? Thus He was divine before, but He bestowed at the time of His Transfiguration a divine power upon the eyes of the apostles and enabled them to look up and see for themselves. The light, then, was not an hallucination but will remain for eternity, and has existed from the beginning.
>
> But if Christ was such and will remain such for eternity, He is also still the same today. It would indeed be absurd to believe that such was His nature up to the most divine vision on Tabor, and that it will always be such in the Age to Come, but that it has become different in the intervening period, setting aside this glory. Today also He is seated in the same splendor, "at the right hand of the Majesty on high." All then must follow and obey Him Who says, "Come, let us ascend the holy and heavenly mountain, let us contemplate the immaterial divinity of the Father and the Spirit, which shines forth in the only Son."[10]

---

8. Maximos the Confessor, "Four Hundred Texts on Love", Palmer, *Philokalia Vol 2*, 69.

9. Palmer, *Philokalia Vol 2*, 74.

10. Palamas, *Triads*, 76.

QUESTIONS FOR TODAY

Gregory challenges us in two particular ways.

Prayer and Perception

How do we actually see the world? In a time of pandemic we become conditioned to look at things in a certain way, through government information (or propaganda), through various media, including newspapers—all give us a lens through which we see things "in a certain light", as we say. But commentators can become jaded or pessimistic. Reading popular *Fox News* in the US or *The Daily Mail* in the UK, for example, gives us a certain slant on things, a certain take, that is not always helpful.

Reflecting on the meaning of Mount Tabor, Gregory raises for us questions about perception: how we look at things, what we actually see. Gregory prompts us to ask: is the glory of God actually in front of our eyes but we just don't see? Have we become blinkered, short-sighted? He is emphatic that the transformation on Tabor was the change in the disciples' eyes and their heightened capacity to see. The key for Gregory in regaining this lost capacity to sense the Divine is the prayer of stillness and silence—this makes possible a state of receptivity enabling a contemplative way of looking at the world. He says in his sermon: "what brought forth this blessed sight was prayer."

A number of recent writers talk of prayer as means of perception and as a way of knowing. Moltmann contrasts two approaches in epistemology. In modern scientific methods, he maintains, we know in order to achieve mastery, to gain possession of our subject. But there is a second way:

> Meditation is in fact an ancient method of arriving at knowledge which has not been pushed aside by our modern activism . . . meditation is pre-eminently a way of sensory perception, of receiving, of absorbing and participating . . . The act of perception transforms the perceiver . . . Perception confers communion. We know in order to participate, not in order to dominate.[11]

For John Macquarrie, prayer helps to heal the human experience of fragmentedness and individualistic isolation, enabling the pray-er to see the world as a whole: "prayer enables us to see things in perspective . . .

---

11. Moltmann, *Spirit of Life*, 200.

Prayer changes our vision of the world . . . Prayer interprets the world."[12] Rowan Williams describes contemplative prayer as involving "the project of reconditioning perception."[13]

Watts and Williams in their study *The Psychology of Religious Knowing* are cautious about assigning a directly cognitive role to prayer, but they recognize significant shifts in perception taking place in the practice of prayer: "Indeed it is doubtful whether the 'acquisition of knowledge' is at all an appropriate way to describe the cognitive changes that take place in prayer. Prayer is probably better described as the *reinterpretation* of what is in some sense already known than as an exercise in the acquisition of knowledge."[14] For Williams and Watts, prayer is "an exercise in the interpretation of experience."[15]

Prayer, especially the quiet, reflective type, becomes the place where real discernment is possible, where we see things with fresh eyes. A. and B. Ulanov in *Primary Speech: A Psychology of Prayer* write of the transformations in perception that can take place in the course of prayer:

> This means we are living now in rearranged form. We are the same persons and yet radically different . . . The theme that dominates our lives now is the effort to correspond with grace. We want to go with the little signs and fragments of new being given us in prayer.[16]

Thus prayer entails the risk of change, in which, little by little, perceptions are revised, self-acceptance grows, and contradictions, if not resolved, become better understood. Effective prayer is, then, not about seeking to influence God, but about allowing God to do extraordinary things in us. This questions our contemporary practice of prayer. It requires of us the ability to silence our own admonitions and advice-giving to God, which can be a feature of intercessory prayer (as if we were advising the Almighty what he should do next). It requires us to come to a place of vulnerability and receptivity before God a wakefulness that the disciples discovered on Tabor.

---

12. Macquarrie, *Paths in Spirituality*, 34.

13. Williams, *Teresa of Avila*, 156.

14. Watts and Williams, *Psychology of Religious Knowing*, 115.

15. Watts and Williams, *Psychology of Religious Knowing*, 113. They find attribution theory helpful in understanding this process, in which religious people attribute events to God.

16. Ulanov, *Primary Speech*, 122. See also experiences of God as understood as perception in Alson, *Perceiving God*.

Gregory prompts us to look again at John's Gospel. The Fourth Gospel does not include an account of the Transfiguration, unlike the other three—perhaps because the themes of perception and transfiguration are on every page. Throughout the fourth gospel, Jesus is seeking eyes wide open. He begins his ministry with the summons, the invitation: "Come and see" (1:39). Jesus wants to open the disciples to a new vision and a fresh way of seeing reality. He calls them to become wide awake to the possibilities God is opening up. He challenges their perception of things. "Do you not say, 'There are yet four months, then comes the harvest'? I tell you, lift up your eyes, and see how the fields are already white for harvest" (John 4:35, RSV). But he is not talking about Samaritan agriculture. The fields around them speak to Jesus of the growth of the Kingdom and the spiritual harvest which has become imminent. In chapter 9 John teaches us about true sight, far deeper than natural eyesight—it is about discerning and recognizing the Divine.

A sacramental way of viewing reality is a dominant theme in the fourth gospel. Jesus sees wine, vines, water, bread, sunlight and candlelight, even shepherding as speaking of himself. Jesus looks at a seed and sees its potential if it perishes: "unless a grain of wheat falls into the earth and dies, it remains just a single grain; but if it dies, it bears much fruit" (12:24). He glimpses his very destiny in a kernel of wheat.

The other gospels combine to give us the clear impression that this was an outlook on the world that was truly characteristic of Jesus himself. The secrets of the Kingdom reveal themselves through parables of seed, mountain, field and sea (Matt 13, Mark 11:23). Jesus says: "Consider the lilies, how they grow . . ." (Luke 12: 27). "Consider": the Greek word means "turn your attention to this, notice what is happening, take note." It is a summons to a contemplative way of life, a deeply reflective way of seeing the world.

Celebrating God's transfiguring power, John invites us to see glory throughout the gospel. What is "glory" in John's perspective? It is the visible radiance of the divine presence—a sign that God is powerfully at work—shining out through human flesh: "And the Word became flesh and lived among us, and we have seen his glory, the glory as of the Father's only Son, full of grace and truth" (1:14).

John even invites us to see problems and even fatal illnesses as situations that are pregnant with the glory of God. Chapter 11 begins with Martha sending an urgent request to Jesus: "Lord, he whom you love is ill." Martha is focusing on the presenting problem; she sees only illness, a brother who is sick. But Jesus is emphatic in his response to Martha's prayer: "This illness does not lead to death; rather it is for God's glory, so that the Son of God may be glorified through it" (11:4). Again, outside Lazarus' tomb Jesus says to Martha: "Did I not tell you that if you believed you would see the glory of God?" (11:40). Martha is invited to pray, not for Lazarus' healing but for the revelation of the glory of God.

All this climaxes at the Cross. Greek pilgrims to Jerusalem declare: "We want to see Jesus" (12:21). He directs them to where they will most clearly see him: "And I, when I am lifted up from the earth, will draw all people to myself" (12:32). The Cross will be not so much an oblation as a revelation: crucifixion becomes glorification, abasement an enthronement. The glory of God is supremely and paradoxically to be revealed on the Cross. While other parts of the New Testament suggest that Jesus first suffers and then receives glory in the resurrection/ascension (Luke 24:26; Heb 2:9), John alone sees the crucifixion of Christ as the greatest moment of transfiguration. In the fourth gospel, Christ can say of his passion: "The hour has come for the Son of Man to be glorified" (12:23; see also 7:39; 13:31; 17:1–5). Jesus approaches his death not as a disaster to be endured, but as a glory to be embraced, for the Cross is the moment of salvation. From the Cross flow forgiveness and hope—it is the greatest hour of God's revelation, the laying bare of his presence. Once again, it is all a matter of looking, of seeing at depth. And like the voice from Tabor, the gospel challenges us to revisit our understanding of perception of the world, and asks us not to place unnecessary limits on our potential.

Deification and Mortality

We live in a time when people's self-worth has been severely undermined by the ravages of a pandemic. Our self-image and understanding of ourselves have become eroded. We are more conscious than ever before of human mortality, vulnerability, finitude, weakness. Many have become demoralized, depressed and pessimistic about the human condition. A healthy self-confidence has been dissolved: we have felt powerless, victims of circumstances, buffeted by things beyond our control. At this very point in time, we need to ascend Mount Tabor and glimpse again an awesome and inspiring view of our unique purpose and being. It is time to recover our lost sense of worth. In a time when personal insecurity threatens to overwhelm us, we need to rediscover our own security in God and celebrate our potentiality. Here is a specific example of changed perception: Tabor opens before us the opportunity to recognize and celebrate God-given powers and glory in each person, rather than only seeing weakness and perishability. Tabor teaches us about honoring our personhood. Tabor—as mediated to us in the voice of Gregory Palamas—restores our dignity, our identity, our sense of sense of purpose:

> The people who walked in darkness
>> have seen a great light;
> those who lived in a land of deep darkness—
>> on them light has shined. (Isa 9:2)

We realize that we are Light-bearers. We celebrate our capacity to welcome the divine energies into every part of our life. Deification is the goal of human existence. At a time when human nature is seen in all its fragility, Gregory offers us the highest possible view of humanity. We may rejoice again in our potentiality: we are made in the image and likeness of God. As Lossky puts it: "I for my part believe that this is the only conception of the Image [of God in humanity] which can fulfil the demands of a Christian anthropology: Man created "in the image" is the person capable of manifesting God in the extent to which his nature allows itself to be penetrated by deifying grace."[17] Gregory celebrates our potentiality:

> He who participates in the divine energy . . . becomes himself, in a sense, Light; he is united to the Light and with the Light he sees in full consciousness all that remains hidden for those who do not have this grace; he thus surpasses not only the corporeal senses, but also all that can be known by the mind . . . for the pure in heart see God . . . who, being the Light, abides in them and reveals Himself to those who love Him, to His beloved ones.[18]

Here below, even in a land of shadow and deep darkness, we can radiate the divine light in our lives—this is why we are here. And we look forward to our eternal destiny, for "the righteous will shine like the sun in the kingdom of their Father" (Matt 13:43).

---

17. Lossky, *Image and Likeness*, 139.

18. Palamas, "Sermon for the Feast of the Presentation of the Blessed Virgin in the Temple", quoted by Lossky, *Image*, 61.

FOR PERSONAL REFLECTION

1. What is your experience of perceptions shifting during the course of prayer? How do you find yourself responding to Gregory's take on the Transfiguration—the change in the disciples' ability to see?

2. What do you make of the observations from Macquarrie, Moltmann and Rowan Williams? Do you agree with them?

3. The glory is always there, seemingly veiled. How can we train ourselves to hone our ability to see deeply, beneath the surface, to recognize the Divine in our very midst, to live in such a way that we might glimpse more of the divinity in the world? God's presence is here before us now—are we seeing it or missing it? How would you assess your own awareness of the Divine?

4. Consider a situation you face right now. See if you can view it differently. Dare you pray: "Lord, show me your glory"?

5. How do you find yourself responding to the affirmation: "Deification is the goal of human existence"?

8

Olivet
Building Hopefulness

> *In hope we were saved.*
> *Now hope that is seen is not hope.*
> *For who hopes for what is seen?*
> *But if we hope for what we do not see,*
> *we wait for it with patience.* (Rom 8:24,25)

THE MOUNT OF OLIVES has always been a place of bold visions, like those of Zechariah and Joel, and in this chapter we meet women who join this tradition of people seeing the bigger picture. Olivet, as it is called, is an extraordinary liminal place: the bridge between the desert and the city, the link between time and eternity, and the intersection between heaven and earth!

Firstly, it is the threshold between the city and the desert, for it marks the ending of the desert and the brink of the city, rising to a height of two and a half thousand feet above sea level. Bethany lies on the eastern flank of the mountain, facing the desert. The western slope of the mountain, just over the crest from Bethany, faces the holy city itself. The Mount of Olives has been called the numinous threshold of the city, for all pilgrims, as they make their journey up from the deep rift valley to the city, must pause at the Mount of Olives, to catch their breath, and to enjoy the amazing panorama of the glistening city below. It is literally and symbolically a watershed: not only does the climate change on this mountain range (desert to the east, Mediterranean type to the west) but also one's very heart and mind change as one climbs the mountain in preparation for the encounter with the holy city.

Secondly, it is the threshold between time and eternity. It is the eschatological mountain, becoming the focus for hopes for God's advent at the end of time. "On that day his feet will stand on the Mount of Olives which lies before Jerusalem on the east; and the Mount of Olives will be spit in two from east to west by a very wide valley" (Zech 14:4). This is the cataclysmic vision of Zechariah in the sixth century before Christ. In a gentler image he had written: "Rejoice greatly, O daughter Zion! Shout aloud O daughter Jerusalem! Lo, your king comes to you; triumphant and victorious is he, humble and riding on a donkey, on a colt, the foal of a donkey" (9:9). In his apocalyptic dream, Joel sees God gathering the nations for judgement in the valley below (Joel 3). So the Mount of Olives becomes a place of judgement and hope in visions of the end of times and here, Jesus gives his "apocalyptic discourse" (Mark 13). To this day, the Mount of Olives is covered with hundreds of tombs: a vast Jewish cemetery clings to its western side, while Christian graves lie in the valley and Muslim tombs stand by the city walls. All three traditions await the coming of God and the dawn of Judgement Day at this location. Humanity's longings for a new world are focused here.[1]

Thirdly, related to these hopes, the Mount of Olives, rising steeply towards the skies, is the threshold between heaven and earth. It is from this summit, according to Luke, that Jesus makes his ascension to the Father in the mysterious cloud, and to which he will return (Luke 24, Acts 1). This is, pre-eminently, the mountain of hope.

From this mountain rise extraordinary women's voices. The Gospels tell us about Martha and Mary and their memorable sayings. In the fourth and fifth centuries two remarkable female pioneers of monastic life ascend the mountain, Melania the Elder and her granddaughter of the same name. As Cohick and Hughes observe: "telling the story of the development of Christianity without women is impossible. Women were on the cutting edge of Christianity's search for place and identity. They contributed substantively to scholarship and the development of practice."[2] As we listen

---

1. Donaldson notes a link between the Mount of Olives (24:3) and the mount of commissioning in Galilee (28:20), with the recurring phrase "the end of the age." Donaldson, *Jesus on the Mountain*.

2. Cohick and Hughes, *Christian Women*, 215.

MELANIA THE ELDER (350–410) discovered this sacred mountain, with all its memories and hopes, to be a magnet for those seeking to get closer to God. Born in Spain to a rich aristocratic family, in 374 she established a community of fifty nuns on its crest, near to the site of the Ascension, and later built a monastery for her friend Rufinus, whom she had got to know in Italy.[3] Melania brings the desert into the city and combines deep prayer, serious study and overflowing compassion. She can be called a Desert Mother because after being widowed at the age of twenty two she left Rome to seek out the blessings of desert monasticism in Nitria (Wadi Natroun) not far from Alexandria in Egypt. Here she learnt much from Abba Macarius and other Desert Fathers. Here she deepened her appreciation of the theological writings of Origen (born c. 185 in Alexandria), which she had come to know through the Latin translations of Rufinus. When persecution broke out after the death of Bishop Athanasius in 373, exiling many of the monks to Diocaesaraea in Palestine, Melania followed and supported them financially from her considerable reserves. Establishing a double monastery on the Mount of Olives, she emerges as a redoubtable spiritual leader and determined pioneer of the monastic experiment.

Four things stand out from her experience on the holy mountain:

1 Commitment to Simplify

Melania renounced her vast wealth or rather utilized it for the development of the church and the poor. She practiced a disciplined asceticism, fasting often and replacing her sumptuous clothes with very simple garb. Her early life in Rome (aged 14–22) as a member of a senatorial family had been sumptuous and indulgent. Now she was learning the art of letting go, travelling light and living simply. She found her divesting of goods liberating for the soul. It is possible that she followed an early version of the Rule of St Basil on the holy mount.[4]

---

3. There are several sources for the life of Melania the Elder, the most complete first-hand record being Palladius, *Lausiac History*; for an older translation see Palladius, *Historia Lausiaca*. Palladius lived for 3 years on the Olivet in the 380s. Translations also in Petersen, *Handmaids of the Lord*.

4. Rufinus translated this into Latin on his return to the West in 400.

On a journey from Jerusalem to Egypt she scolded deacon Juvinus who, in intense heat, treated himself to a bodywash in cold water:

> How can a warm-blooded young man like you dare to pamper your flesh that way? Do you not know that this is the source of much harm? Look, I am sixty years old and neither my feet nor my face, nor any of my members, except for the tips of my fingers, has touched water, although I am afflicted with many ailments and my doctors urge me. I have not yet made concessions to my bodily desires, nor have I used a couch for resting, nor have I ever made a journey on a litter![5]

Aged sixty, she traveled to Rome, promoting and teaching the ascetic, peace-loving life. Among those choosing to follow her in the practice of self-control and renunciation were her daughter-in-law Albina, her granddaughter Melania the Younger and her husband, Pinianus. She challenged the Roman senators and their wives, for whom notions of asceticism within marriage, chastity, and virginity were deeply scandalous. Palladius records her prophetic response:

> *Little children,* it was written over four hundred years ago, *it is the last hour.* Why are you fond of the vain things of life? Beware lest the days of the Antichrist overtake you and you not enjoy your wealth and your ancestral property.[6]

Her words were prophetic, for Rome was soon sacked by Alaric in 410, the year of her repose.

2 Dedication to Learning

Melania the Elder had a great love of reading and study. Palladius tells us, perhaps with exaggeration, that she read three million lines of Origen, two and a half million lines of such writers as Basil of Caesarea and Gregory, and, of Scripture commentaries, the equivalent of three times the volume of Homer's Iliad. Fluent and well read in both Latin and Greek, she developed a substantial library on the Mount of Olives, but her serious commitment to study was not an end in itself—it somehow fueled her ministry of outreach, and equipped her for her missions. Palladius puts it: "Thus it was possible for her to be liberated from knowledge so-called and to mount on

---

5. Palladius, *History*, 136.
6. Palladius, *History* 135.

wings, thanks to these books—by good hopes she transformed herself into a spiritual bird and so made the journey to Christ."[7]

Melania the Elder's social network was one of the most important in the fourth and early fifth century Christianity, her connections reaching from Spain to Persia. As part of the first generation of the nobility taking Christianity seriously, she lived to see it become the official religion of the Empire. In the difficult period between the Councils of Nicaea and Chalcedon, Melania and her community on the Mount of Olives became a significant center of learning, wisdom and pastoral care. It was a place of stability and humble study in an unpredictable world. She used her theological knowledge too in helping to restore the fractured unity of Christians who were being torn apart by controversy. As Palladius puts it: "They edified all their visitors and united the four hundred monks of the Pauline schism by persuading every heretic who denied the Holy Spirit and so brought them back to the Church." [8] Melania refused to be defeated by divisive circumstances in the church and had the gift of seeing opportunity in difficulty.

3 Compassion for Poor and Ministry of Hospitality

On the holy mountain Melania offers us an inspiring model of hospitality. Palladius tells us that Melania had already supported thousands of Egyptian monks who had been threatened by the emperor, providing food and refuge to those fleeing persecution and giving practical encouragement to those arrested. The depth of her compassion for the needy is reflected in an Egyptian tradition holding that to alleviate suffering at the hands of the Arians, she fed out of her own wealth some 5,000 people over the course of three days.

When the monks were exiled to Palestine she disguised herself with a slave's garb in order to smuggle out provisions to hungry hermits under the cover of darkness. When imprisoned for doing this, she said to the Consul of Diocaesaraea: "I am So-and-so's daughter and So-and-so's wife? I am Christ's slave. Pray do not look down upon my shabby clothes, for I could make more of myself if I would!"[9] When the judge realized her social status, he let her go. The *Lausiac History* records that Melania used her own money to help churches, monasteries, refugees, and prisoners throughout

---

7. Palladius, *History* 136, 137.
8. Palladius, *History,* 124.
9. Palladius, *History,*124.

the Empire, as well as in Persia.[10] Palladius tells us: "For twenty-seven years they [Melania and Rufinus] both entertained with their own private funds the bishops, solitaries, and virgins who visited them, coming to Jerusalem to fulfill a vow . . . They bestowed gifts on the local clergy, and so finished their days without offending anyone."[11]

Melania found herself standing in the tradition of Martha and Mary in the way she offered hospitality, welcome and support, much as those sisters did to Jesus at Bethany just over the crest of the Mount of Olives, aided by their own Rufinus, brother Lazarus.

4 Ministry of Encouragement and Fostering Vocations

Melania spent much of those twenty-seven years on the Mount of Olives dedicated to supporting people in their religious quest. Her most famous protégé was EVAGRIUS OF PONTUS (345–99) who was destined to become a leader of desert monasticism. She became a spiritual mentor to him when he arrived in Jerusalem in 382 wearied physically and spiritually. He had fled to Jerusalem from Constantinople, where he had strayed into some involvement with a married woman. Palladius tells us: "He wished to break off with the woman, who by now was eager and frantic, but he could not do so, so caught up was he in the bonds of concupiscence."[12] With a rare combination of fierceness and compassion Melania counselled him at this crucial time in his life when he was questioning his vocation and struggling spiritually. When he arrived in the holy city he was still besotted with his appearance and clothes and suffering from proud self-preoccupation and vainglory. He fell seriously ill and only after he shared his troubles with Melania, and accepted her guidance about becoming a monk, was he restored to health. Palladius records these words of encouragement to Evagrius from Melania:

> Promise me by the Lord that you mean to aim at the monastic life, and even though I am a sinner, I will pray that you be given a lease on life.[13]

---

10. Palladius, *History*, 134.
11. Palladius, *History*, 124.
12. Palladius, *History*, 111.
13. Palladius, *History*, 113.

Olivet

She supported him a crucial and formative period in his life and helped him to clarify his very purpose and vocation. She herself clothed him in monastic garb when he made the decision to follow the ascetic life. When he retired to Nitrea in Lower Egypt to pursue the monastic life in 385, Melania became an important link in the evolution of the ascetic movement, for Evagrius went on to flourish as an influential teacher of prayer and gifted theologian, playing a key role in the development of monasticism in the East. His time on the Mount of Olives was not only an experience of renewal and healing—he clarified his calling on the holy mountain and deepened his understanding of prayer. On his move to a community of monks in Nitria and later to a monastery in Kellia, Evagrius continued his spiritual friendship with Melania through correspondence.[14] We do not have her letters to him, but he writes to her appreciatively: "Like cool waters for a thirsty soul, so are good tidings to a distant land . . .The letters you sent beautifully quench the fire that comes upon us from toils, as did those others you wrote, that your Excellence sent to us before. For everything that is useful to our honor and our refreshment you provide from your whole soul."[15] He composed an infamous Letter to Melania which was Origenist in content, revealing his attraction for ideas of pre-existence from Origen.[16]

Later he wrote for Rufinus, who had been both spiritual guide and physician in his time on the Mount of Olives, a hundred and fifty three short *Chapters on Prayer* which distill his experience of prayer that Olivet had helped to shape:

> Prayer is the fruit of joy and thanksgiving.
> Prayer is the exclusion of sadness and despondency.
> Go, sell your possessions and give to the poor, and take up your cross so that you can pray without distraction.
> Do not be over-anxious and strain yourself so as to gain an immediate hearing for your request. The Lord wishes to confer greater favors than those you ask for, in reward for your perseverance. For what greater thing is there than to converse intimately with God and to be pre-occupied with his company?
> Prayer is an ascent of the spirit to God.

---

14. See Young, "A Life in Letters."

15. Letter 37:1 quoted in Young, "The Role of Letters," 163.

16. Evagrius (trans. Parmentier), *Letter to Melania*. Online translation by Luke Dysinger.

Evagrius also wrote for Melania *Mystic Sentences* or *Mirror for Monks and Nuns*, translated by Rufinus into Latin. Migne, *Patrologia Graeca* 40: 1277–86.

> If you are a theologian you truly pray. If you truly pray you are a theologian.
>
> The Holy Spirit takes compassion on our weakness, and though we are impure he often comes to visit us. If he should find our spirit praying to him out of love for the truth he then descends upon it and dispels the whole army of thoughts and reasonings that beset it. And too he urges it on to the works of spiritual prayer.[17]

Other examples of the personal support given by Melania abound. When at the age of sixty she travelled to Rome, she nurtured into faith her cousin's husband Apronianus. It was on this visit, we noted, that she encouraged her granddaughter about a religious calling, The Younger ultimately following her grandmother back to Jerusalem.

RUFINUS (340–410) beckons us to meet him more fully. Born near Aquileia on the Adriatic's northern shore, at the age of thirty he was living in a monastic community here when he first met Jerome and they became friends. In about 372, Rufinus moved to Alexandria and met up with Macarius the Elder and other ascetics in the desert and he followed Melania when she fled to Palestine in the persecutions. In 380 Rufinus took charge of a community of monks on Olivet, next to Melania's own convent. Devoting himself to the study of Greek theology, he combined the contemplative life and the life of learning which he had seen modeled in the Egyptian monasteries. When Jerome came to Bethlehem in 386, the friendship formed at Aquileia was renewed, but later they fell out over different interpretations of Origen's controversial ideas about pre-existent souls falling into their bodies, and the renewal of all things (*apokatastasis*). Returning to Rome in 397, Rufinus spent much of his time translating Origen and other works, including Eusebius' *Ecclesiastical History*. We can hardly overestimate the influence which Rufinus exerted on Western theologians by thus putting the great Greek fathers into the Latin tongue.[18]

On Olivet no doubt Rufinus participated in the liturgies of the Ascension which Egeria describes in 384.[19] The first church on the site was

---

17. Evagrius, *Praktis*, chapters 15, 16, 17, 34, 35, 60, 62. Also in Palmer, *Philokalia* Vol 1.

18. Between 397 and 408 he lived in Rome and Aquileia; in 408 Rufinus was at the monastery of Pinetum in the Campagna, driven there by Alaric's arrival in northern Italy. He fled to Sicily in the company of Melania the Younger when Alaric moved south and pillaged Rome in 410. He died in Sicily in 411.

19. Gingras, *Egeria: Diary*, 119.

Olivet

built before 392, known as the *Imbomon* (Greek for "on the hill"). Rufinus lived on the Mount of Olives 380–397 so he witnessed the construction of the first rotunda—a structure with no roof, totally open to the summoning heavens, surrounded by circular porticos and arches (the Crusaders remodeled it into the octagonal domed structure we see today). In those seventeen years on the holy mountain Rufinus had opportunity to ponder deeply the mystery of the resurrection and ascension, and he embodies these insights in his Commentary on the Apostles' Creed:

> *The Third Day He Rose Again from the Dead.* The glory of Christ's resurrection threw a luster upon everything which before had the appearance of weakness and frailty. If a while since it seemed to you impossible that an immortal Being could die, you see now that He who has overcome death and is risen again cannot be mortal. But understand herein the goodness of the Creator, that so far as you by sinning have cast yourself down, so far has He descended in following you... The flesh which had been deposited in the sepulcher, is raised, that that might be fulfilled which was spoken by the Prophet, "You will not suffer Your Holy One to see corruption." He returned, therefore, a victor from the dead, leading with Him the spoils of hell. For He led forth those who were held in captivity by death, as He Himself had foretold, when He said, "When I shall be lifted up from the earth I shall draw all unto Me."
>
> Sitting, therefore, on the right hand of God in the highest heavens, He placed there that human flesh, made perfect through sufferings, which had fallen to death by the lapse of the first man, but was now restored by the virtue of the resurrection. The Apostle says, "Who has raised us up together and made us sit together in the heavenly places." For He was the potter, Who, as the Prophet Jeremiah teaches, took up again with His hands, and formed anew, as it seemed good to Him, the vessel which had fallen from His hands and was broken in pieces. And it seemed good to Him that the mortal and corruptible body which He had assumed, this body raised from the rocky sepulcher and rendered immortal and incorruptible, He should now place not on the earth but in heaven, and at His Father's right hand...
>
> *He Ascended into Heaven, and Sits on the Right Hand of the Father: from Thence He Shall Come to Judge the Living and the Dead.* What is said is plain, but the question is how and in what sense it is to be understood. For to ascend, and to sit, and to come, unless you

understand the words in accordance with the dignity of the divine nature, appear to point to something of human weakness. For having consummated what was to be done on earth, and having recalled souls from the captivity of hell, He is spoken of as ascending up to heaven, as the Prophet had foretold, "Ascending up on high He led captivity captive, and gave gifts unto all", those gifts, namely, which Peter, in the Acts of the Apostles, spoke of concerning the Holy Spirit, "Being therefore by the right hand of God exalted, He has shed forth this gift which you do see and hear." He gave the gift of the Holy Spirit to all, because the captives, whom the devil had before carried into hell through sin, Christ by His resurrection from death recalled to heaven. He ascended therefore into heaven, not where God the Word had not been before, for He was always in heaven, and abode in the Father, but where the Word made flesh had not been seated before . . .

To sit at the right hand of the Father is a mystery belonging to the Incarnation. For it does not befit that incorporeal nature without the assumption of flesh; neither is the excellency of a heavenly seat sought for the divine nature, but for the human. It is said of Him, "Your seat, O God, is prepared from eternity; You are from everlasting." The seat, then, on which the Lord Jesus was to sit, was prepared from everlasting, "in Whose name every knee should bow, of things in heaven and things on earth, and things under the earth; and every tongue shall confess to Him that Jesus is Lord in the glory of God the Father"; of Whom also David thus speaks, "The Lord said to my Lord, Sit on my right hand until I make Your enemies Your footstool". . .

That He shall come to judge the living and the dead we are taught by many testimonies of the divine Scriptures . . . we think it necessary to remind you that this doctrine of the faith would have us daily solicitous concerning the coming of the Judge, that we may so frame our conduct as having to give account to the Judge who is at hand.[20]

MELANIA THE YOUNGER (383–439) like her grandmother sharing both the same name and the same aristocratic heritage, was at once formidable and big-hearted. Born at Rome, she married Pinianus a patrician, but after the death of her two children they resolved to live as brother and sister

---

20. Rufinus, "Commentary on the Apostles' Creed", *Life and Works*, paragraphs 29, 31, 32, 33. The Commentary was composed in 407.

and embark on a quest to find a life of prayer. The invasions of Italy by the Visigoths, together with the encouragement of her grandmother, occasioned the start of this spiritual adventure, and she left Rome in 410. After two years in Sicily she went to Africa where she and Pinianus shared a monastic life for seven years, founding a convent, during which time she grew well acquainted with St Augustine of Hippo. In 417, Melania and Pinianus traveled to Palestine by way of Alexandria. On arrival in the holy city she enrolled on the register of poor people, wanting her wealth to be undiscovered and wishing to live in poverty whilst utilizing her resources for the support of the church. Like her grandmother, Melania the Younger was drawn to the mystical Mount of Olives and she also went on to build both a convent for women and, later, a monastery for men charged with the responsibility to maintain unbroken praise in the place of the Ascension of Christ through the day and night. Her constructions were located between Constantine's *Eleona* Church, built above the traditional cave where Jesus gave his end-time teaching (Matthew 23–26) and the Church of the Ascension, the *Imbomon*. Situated at the crest of the sacred mountain, from this vantage point her monks and nuns could look west to the bustle and passion of the holy city or east to the silent hills of the desert. Later she built a further chapel nearby saying:

> This is the place in which the feet of the Lord stood. Therefore let us build here a holy oratory, so that after my journey from this world to the Lord an offering on behalf of my soul and those of my masters can also be offered unceasingly in this place.[21]

A colleague on the Mount of Olives for twenty seven years, and placed in charge of the men's monastery through this period was Gerontius, the priest who wrote a biography and gives us some of her sayings. Melania was unknown for centuries in the West but in the last century or so two manuscripts of her *Vita* have been rediscovered: a Latin version found by Cardinal Rampolla in 1884 in the Vatican library and a Greek codex by the Bollandists in the Barberini Library, Rome.[22] These enable us to hear the voice of Melania the Younger today.

Melania the Younger was a compassionate and resolute person. With her sisters she was considerate and understanding, making allowances for those struggling with fasting or lack of sleep, for example. Her modesty and

---

21. Clark, *Life of Melania the Younger*, 69.

22. Rampolla tells the story of the manuscripts and gives his view of Melania the Younger in Rampolla del Tindaro, *Life of St Melania*.

humility were evident when elected to the office of superior in her community—she stepped aside in deference to others. She replaced her former silks with haircloth, concealed under her garb, and was committed to the discipline of fasting to deepen prayer. She had high expectations of her sisters:

> Sisters, recall how the subjected stand before their mortal and worldly rulers with all fear and vigilance; so we who stand before the fearsome and heavenly King should perform our liturgy with much fear and trembling. Just keep in mind that neither the angels nor any intelligible or heavenly creature can worthily praise the Lord who needs nothing and is beyond praise. If then the incorporeal powers, who so much surpass our nature, fall short in worthily celebrating the God of all things . . . how much more ought we, useless servants, to sing psalms in all fear and trembling, lest we bring judgement upon ourselves for our lack of care in glorifying our Master instead of reward and benefit.
>
> As for pure love to him and to each other, we are taught by the Holy Scriptures that we ought to guard it with all zeal, recognizing that without spiritual love all discipline and virtue is in vain. [The devil] is conquered by love and by humility . . . Let us flee the vainglory of this age that fades like a plant's flower. And before all else let us guard the holy and orthodox faith without deviation, for this is the groundwork and the foundation of our whole life in the Lord. Let us love the holiness of our souls and bodies because apart from this, no one will see the Lord.[23]

She told this story to teach about bearing trouble and not retaliating:

> Someone went to an aged holy man wanting to be instructed by him, and the holy man said to him, "Can you obey me in everything for the sake of the Lord?" And he answered the father, "I will do everything that you order me with great zeal." The holy man said, "Take a scourge, go over to that place, and hit and kick that statue." The man returned having willing done what he was commanded. The old man said to him, "Did the statue protest or answer back while it was being struck or kicked?" And he replied, "Not at all." The father said "Then go again, hit it a second time and add insults as well." When he had done this still a third time at the command of the father and the statue did not answer—for how could it, since it was stone?—then at last the old saint said to him,

---

23. Clark, *Melania the Younger*, 56, 57.

Olivet

"If you can become like that statue, insulted but not returning the insult, struck but not protesting, then you can also be saved and remain with me." Let us too, O children, imitate this statue and nobly submit to everything—to insult, reproach, contempt—in order that we may inherit the Kingdom of Heaven.[24]

Melania the Younger's life on the Mount of Olives is permeated with hopefulness. She is confident about the potential for spiritual growth in her religious sisters. She believes in their capacity to deepen their experience of God. She keeps vigil in her prayers with a sense of expectancy and faith. And, living on this threshold between heaven and earth, in the very place where Jesus ascends to heaven and to which believers trust he will return, she keeps her sights set on the world to come. Gerontius tells us that Melania, approaching her deathbed, left her sisters this "spiritual testament":

> I exhort you to be eager after my departure to perform the office in fear and vigilance . . . If I am to be separated from you in body in a short while and will no longer be with you, God who is eternal and fulfils all things will dwell with you, and he knows the depths of every heart. Thus have him before your eyes constantly and keep your souls in love and purity to the end, knowing that all of us must appear before his fearsome throne . . .

And Gerontius gives us Melania's final prayer:

> God, the Lord of the holy martyrs, who knows all things before they come to pass, you know what I chose from the beginning, that I love you with all my heart . . . For I have given my soul and body to you, who formed me in my mother's womb, and you have taken my right hand to guide me in your counsel . . . Therefore accept my prayer which I offer to you with these tears, through the intercession of your holy athletes [martyrs], and purify me, your servant, so that in my coming to you, the steps of my soul may be unfettered . . . that I may go to you spotless, guided by your holy angels. May I be deemed worthy of your heavenly bridal chamber when I have heard your blessed voice, by which you will say to those who please you, "Come, the blessed of my Father, inherit the kingdom prepared for you from the creation of the world." For to you belongs inexpressible compassion and abundant pity; you will save all those who hope in you.[25]

---

24. Clark, *Melania the Younger*, 58.
25. Clark, *Melania the Younger*, 77.

Melania then fell asleep in the Lord, 31 December 439, on the sacred mountain of hope.

QUESTIONS FOR TODAY

The Covid and post-Covid world can sometimes seem like a place of despondency and fearfulness. During the pandemic many have suffered mental health problems and low esteem, fueling depression, a sense of negativity and hopelessness. The voices of the Mount of Olives hearten us and challenge us in such times. They brim with a kind of hopefulness that refuses fatalism, that rejects determinism, and is ready to experiment and break boundaries. The outlook revealed by the two Melanias and Rufinus testifies to a radical hope that never gives in, that dares to look beyond limits—a hopefulness that overcomes barriers, glimpsing possibilities, both in this world and the next. It is unafraid of failure and refuses to be defeated by difficult circumstances. It is ready to envision new futures, visualizing alternatives, seeing new creative paths ahead. Caroline T. Schroeder observes of the *Life of Melania the Younger*: "Melania the monastic serves as a hagiographic model for expressing *eupatheiai*, good feelings. Her otherwise controlled demeanor is regularly punctuated by moments of zeal, desire and joy, which are almost always coded as virtuous . . . .According to Gerontius . . . her heart 'burned even more strongly with the divine fire.'"[26]

The two Melanias were pioneers. On the Mount of Olives, with their double monasteries, they were extending the monastic experiment and doing so in a man's world. Indeed Palladius says that the Elder was recognized as "a female man of God."[27] Women won't supposed to do these kind of things. They were supposed to accept the status quo and bend the knee in obedience to abbots and bishops and husbands, but the Melanias refused to be hemmed in by prevailing gender stereotypes. They were ready to break the mold.

Such an outlook had manifested itself in the women before they came to the holy mount. In Rome they refused to be trapped into conventional aristocratic life: they wanted to break free and choose their own path. They scandalized their families by their renunciation and giving away of vast resources. Both Melanias, in their different ways, smashed stereotypes of women, escaping straightjackets of inherited conventions, rejecting

---

26. "Exemplary Women," 58.
27. Palladius, *History*, 43.

traditional expectations about the roles of mother and wife, and so were able to reclaim their lives and forge new futures. Their hopefulness revealed itself in discernment and decisiveness. The Melanias found that letting go of material attachments was liberating, freeing them for a ministry of availability and unrestricted discipleship.

Nor could Melania the Elder be typecast as a regular pious humble pilgrim to the Holy Land. After researching desert monasticism in Egypt, she entered Palestine as a fearless pioneer, saying in effect "if the men can do it in Egypt I can do it in Palestine!" En route, at Diocaesaraea, she was prepared to stand up to the pomposity of the consul, and even poke fun at him. The Younger was undeterred in her efforts to change the religious skyline of the Mount of Olives and developed her monastic complexes without hesitation. As we noted, she believed in her sisters' potentiality, rather than their limitations, and so nurtured and spurred them onto spiritual growth. She reveals a confident belief in their increasing capacity for the Divine.

Both feisty women were prepared to take on theological giants of their day and not be subject to theological bullying or narrow-mindedness. They were unafraid of controversy. The Elder and Rufinus dared to clash with Jerome over interpretations of Origen while the Younger was even ready to question Augustine on the views of Pelagius![28]

What is the source of their hopefulness, courage and verve that might hearten us today? What equipped and made possible their outlook? What inspired their synergy with the Divine, a partnership between their material resources and their God-given vision? What nurtured their quiet inner authority that revealed itself in a rare combination of humility and determination? It is Rufinus who puts this most eloquently in his reflections on the Creed, which he begins with the words:

> *I Believe*, therefore, is placed in the forefront, as the Apostle Paul, writing to the Hebrews, says, "He that comes to God must first of all believe that He is, and that He is a rewarder of those who believe in Him." The Prophet also says, "Unless you believe, you shall not understand." That the way to understand, therefore, may be open to you, you do rightly first of all, in professing that you believe; for no one embarks upon the sea, and trusts himself to the deep and liquid element, unless he first believes it possible that he will have a safe voyage; neither does the husbandman commit his seed to the furrows and scatter his grain on the earth, but in the belief that the showers will come, together with the sun's warmth,

28. She met with Pelagius in Palestine in 418.

through whose fostering influence, aided by favoring winds, the earth will produce and multiply and ripen its fruits. Nothing in life can be transacted if there be not first a readiness to believe.[29]

The word "confidence", of course, means literally "with faith." Rufinus and the Melanias were motivated by an unshakable faith and trust in a God who in incarnation comes to share our frailty and who in ascension from the holy mount lifts our humanity to the heights of heaven.

FOR PERSONAL REFLECTION

1. What parts of the experience of the two Melanias inspire you most in your current situation?
2. Both Melania the Elder and the Younger, standing in the tradition of Martha and Mary, give generous hospitality on the holy mountain, and their foundations provided a center of stillness in a fractured world. Where do you turn for support?
3. Is anything holding you back from creativity and initiative?
4. Rufinus concludes his thoughts on the Ascension and return of Christ with the comment "this doctrine of the faith would have us daily solicitous concerning the coming of the Judge, that we may so frame our conduct as having to give account to the Judge who is at hand." Can you think of other examples of doctrine having an impact on lived human behavior?
5. What do you think, is the difference between optimism and hope? How can we increase hopefulness?
6. How can the resurrection and ascension of Jesus become the cornerstone to a worldview that provides the perspective to all of life?

---

29. Rufinus, "Commentary on the Apostles' Creed," *Life and Works*, paragraph 1.

9

Calvary
Resourcing Courage

> *The stone that the builders rejected*
>   *has become the chief cornerstone.*
> *This is the Lord's doing;*
>   *it is marvelous in our eyes.* (Ps 118:22,23)

FROM THE BEGINNING, IN the distant mists of time, the two mountains looked at each other across the valley. Eyeing each other up, they wondered about their respective destinies. In themselves they were not the most impressive mountains in the world—no Everest or Mount Fuji. But these two unprepossessing and unassuming hills were to become for a large part of the globe's population the most sacred, cosmic mountains on the planet. The high place of Zion atop the Ophel Ridge was to bear the very presence of the Divine, represented in the Ark, while opposite, amidst a rough quarried area of limestone cliffs, Mount Calvary, Golgotha, the place of the skull, was destined to be the locus of the world's salvation. Two symbols of the Divine were to face each other across the Tyropoeon Valley that runs north-south through the center of Jerusalem: Temple and Cross.

Looking at the temple Jesus realized precisely what God was calling him to. He knew the Scriptures—the call of the Jerusalem prophet

Calvary

Jeremiah, with whom he closely identified:[1] "I have called you to destroy and overthrow, to build and to plant" (Jer 1:10). Jesus knew the words of Ecclesiastes: there is "a time to break down and a time to build up" (3:3). And so, standing within the temple precincts, Jesus says: "Destroy this temple, and in three days I will raise it up" (John 2:19). There was an outcry: "The Jews then said, 'This temple has been under construction for forty six years, and will you raise it up in three days?'" John adds: "but he was speaking of the temple of his body" (2: 19–21). For Jesus, Zion points to the mount of Calvary.

It is significant that Jesus is killed in a quarry.[2] The rock of Calvary itself may have been left standing amidst the ancient quarry outside the city wall precisely because it was useless—a deep fracture running from its top into the earth indicates that it was unsuitable for use in building—it became a rejected rock, scarred and shattered. In Matthew's gospel, Sinai-like earthquakes attend both the crucifixion and resurrection: "the earth shook and the rocks were split" (Matt 27:51, see also 28:2). The rock of Calvary is indeed battered and bruised to this day: its deep scar and fracture speaks powerfully of the woundedness and vulnerability of Christ.

The first Christians, seeking to make sense of the event of Calvary, turned to the Hebrew Scriptures and there they found texts which spoke of a rejected rock being used in God's rebuilding purposes for humanity: "The very stone that the builders rejected has become the cornerstone." This verse from the psalms (118:22) is used by different communities in the New Testament (quoted in Mark, Matthew, Luke in the Holy Week story, by Peter in his sermon to the Acts 4:11, and by the writer of 1 Peter 2:7). Jesus is also understood as "a stone one strikes against, a rock one stumbles over" (Isa 8:14–15). But such a stone becomes the keystone in the new work, the new temple which God is building, for a further text from Isaiah inspired the first Christians: "See, I am laying in Zion a foundation stone, a tested stone, a precious cornerstone, a sure foundation" (28:16). This is quoted in Romans (9:33) and 1 Peter (2:4–6). The rock of Golgotha, standing to this day, is at once a memorial to the crucifixion and a pointer to a new future.

Today, the rock of Calvary is part of a complex in the Church of the Holy Sepulcher that makes up "the rock of our salvation." The Gospel accounts of the first Easter specifically mention the rock of the mountain. There is the tomb itself which Joseph of Arithamea had had cut into the

---

1. Jesus quotes Jeremiah 7:11 at the "cleansing of the temple" in Mark 11:17.
2. Biddle, *Holy Sepulcher*; Need, *Jerusalem: Church of the Holy Sepulchre.*

rock-cliff (*petra*). There is the mighty rock or *lithos* that attempted to seal the tomb of Christ and was blasted away in the resurrection events (according to Matthew: parts are preserved in the antechamber of the tomb today in the Altar of the Angels).

The Rock of Calvary, the apex of the craggy hill, was crowned by a statue of Venus or Aphrodite by Hadrian when he Romanized the city of Jerusalem in AD 135. He gave the city a new name Aelia Capitolina (thereby dedicating the rebuilt city to Jupiter Capitolinus) and wished to stamp out all previous religious devotions where they were flourishing. He erected a shrine to Jupiter on the Temple Mount, amidst the ruins of the temple, and, on a seemingly insignificant hill, (which had been outside the city walls but brought within them by Agrippa in AD 42 when he expanded them) he placed a marble deity, covering the Tomb nearby with soil and with a platform supporting a new temple and agora. After Constantine became a Christian, his mother Helena came to the Holy Land to erect great Christian basilicas in places of significance, but first she had to organize an excavation, because the Tomb of Christ was now below ground and the summit of Calvary was surrounded by pagan structures. In his *Life of Constantine* the historian of the early church Eusebius of Caesarea (265–339) gives us a vivid account of the discovery of the tomb and the re-emergence of the Rock. The stone which the builders rejected was truly becoming the cornerstone of something astonishing on Mount Calvary:

> The Emperor Constantine decided that he ought to make universally famous and revered the most blessed site in Jerusalem of the Savior's resurrection. So at once he gave orders for a place of worship to be constructed, conceiving this idea not without God, but with his spirit moved by the Savior himself.
>
> Once upon a time wicked men, or rather the whole tribe of demons through them, had striven to consign to darkness and oblivion that divine monument to immortality . . . It was this very cave of the Savior that some godless and wicked people had planned to make invisible to mankind, thinking in their stupidity that they could in this way hide the truth. Indeed with a great expenditure of effort they brought earth from somewhere outside and covered up the whole place, then levelled it, paved it, and so hid the divine cave somewhere down beneath a great quantity of soil. Then as though they had everything finished, above the ground they constructed a terrible and truly genuine tomb, one for souls, for dead idols, and built a gloomy sanctuary to the impure

Calvary

demon of Aphrodite; then they offered foul sacrifices there upon defiled and polluted altars . . .

At a word of command [from Constantine] those contrivances of fraud were demolished from top to bottom, and the houses of error were dismantled and destroyed along with their idols and demons . . . the Emperor gave instructions that the site should be excavated to a great depth . . .

As stage by stage the underground site was exposed, at last against all expectation the revered and all hallowed Testimony (*martyrion*) of the Savior's resurrection was itself revealed, and the cave, the holy of holies, took on the appearance of a representation of the Savior's return to life. Thus after its descent into darkness it came forth again to the light, and it enabled those who came as visitors to see plainly the story of the wonders wrought there, testifying by facts louder than any voice to the resurrection of the Savior.

With these things thus completed, the Emperor next gave orders by the stipulations of pious laws and by generous grants for a place of worship of God to be built with rich and imperial munificence around the Savior's cave . . . He instructed those who governed the eastern provinces by generous and lavish grants to make the building out of the ordinary, huge, and rich . . .[3]

Constantine went on to construct both a stunning basilica to the east and a beautiful structure around the Tomb (which he separated from the surrounding rock)—between these, now in a paved court, rose the mysterious and evocative Rock of Calvary.[4] Who was present at the excavation and the discovery of the Tomb, a stone's throw away from the Rock? The Secretary of the Palestine Exploration Fund, writing in 1890, surmises:

While the temple of Venus with its foundations was being cleared away . . . was probably present a Christian lad, native of Jerusalem, eleven years of age, watching the discovery . . . of the rock containing the sacred tomb. It was Cyril, afterwards Bishop of Jerusalem

---

3. Cameron and Hall, *Life of Constantine*, 133.
4. The Crusaders incorporated all the sites under one roof of a Romanesque church—this is what we see today. We get a clear sense of ascending the hill of Calvary today because the Via Dolorosa, the Way of the Cross, makes a steep ascent up many steps, and there is a flight of steps to climb inside the Church of the Holy Sepulcher, to the chapel now to be found at the top of Calvary. There one can see and touch the living rock of Calvary.

> ... One must not forget ... that though he was a boy at the time of the discovery, he lived in Jerusalem and must have watched, step by step, the progress of the great Basilica; that he was ordained before the completion and dedication of the buildings. And that many, if not all, of his lectures were delivered in the Church of the *Anastasis* itself.[5]

CYRIL OF JERUSALEM (315–86), a priest working for the Church of the Resurrection, prepared candidates for baptism at this very spot by the Rock: his *Catechetical Lectures* (350) communicate to us, even now, his sense of wonderment and delight at standing on the holy hill and leading others into the Mysteries:

> Many, my beloved, are the true testimonies concerning Christ. The Father bears witness from heaven of His Son; the Holy Spirit bears witness, descending bodily in likeness of a dove; the Archangel Gabriel bears witness, bringing good tidings to Mary ... Golgotha, the holy hill standing above us here, bears witness to our sight; the Holy Sepulcher bears witness, and the stone which lies there to this day ...[6]
>
> He was truly crucified for our sins. For if you would deny it, the place refutes you visibly, this blessed Golgotha, in which we are now assembled for the sake of Him who was here crucified.[7]
>
> Jesus then really suffered for all; for the Cross was no illusion, otherwise our redemption is an illusion also ...[8] His passion then was real: for He was really crucified, and we are not ashamed at that; He was crucified and we do not deny it, no, I rather glory to speak of it. For though I should now deny it, here is Golgotha to refute me, near which we are now assembled; the wood of the Cross confutes me which was afterwards distributed piecemeal from here to all the world. I confess the Cross because I know of the Resurrection ... the Resurrection has followed the Cross, I am not ashamed to declare it.[9]

---

5. Besant, "Holy Sepulcher", 115.

6. Gifford, "Cyril of Jerusalem", Lecture X:19. The text has been modernized, changing "thee" and "thou" into "you."

7. Gifford, "Cyril of Jerusalem", Lecture XIII:4.

8. Referring to the Docetists.

9. Gifford, "Cyril of Jerusalem", Lecture IV:10.

Calvary

> We can never be tired of hearing concerning the crowning [with thorns] of our Lord, and least of all in this most holy Golgotha. For others only hear, but we both see and handle. Let none be weary; take your armor against the adversaries in the cause of the Cross itself...[10]

> He stretched out His hands on the Cross, that He might embrace the ends of the world; for this Golgotha is the very center of the earth.[11]

> These cry out to you: this holy Golgotha, which stands high above us, and shows itself to this day, and displays even still how because of Christ the rocks were then riven; the sepulcher near at hand where He was laid, and the stone which was laid on the door, which lies to this day by the tomb.[12]

What is the meaning of the crucifixion for Cyril? He takes his cue from the physical setting of the cross and tomb: the garden (mentioned in John 19:41) evokes Paradise lost and regained through the Cross. Physicality reveals spirituality and earthly topographical features point to heavenly realities:

> Adam received the sentence, "Cursed is the ground in your labors; thorns and thistles shall it bring forth to you" [Gen 3:17,18]. For this cause Jesus assumes the thorns, that He may cancel the sentence; for this cause also was He buried in the earth, that the earth which had been cursed might receive the blessing instead of a curse... And since we have touched on things concerning Paradise, I am truly astonished at the truth of the types. In Paradise was the Fall, and in a Garden was our salvation. From the Tree came sin, and until the Tree sin lasted. In the evening, when the Lord walked in the Garden, they hid themselves; and in the evening the robber is brought by the Lord into Paradise... [Christ says:] "Truly I say unto you, this day you shall be with me in Paradise [Luke 23:43] because 'Today you have heard My voice, and have not hardened your heart' [Ps 95:7,8]. Very speedily I passed sentence upon Adam, very speedily I pardon you... Adam by the Tree fell away; you by the Tree are brought into Paradise... Of this garden I sang of old to My spouse in the Canticles...: 'I am

---

10. Gifford, "Cyril of Jerusalem", Lecture XIII: 22.
11. Gifford, "Cyril of Jerusalem", Lecture XIII: 28.
12. Gifford, "Cyril of Jerusalem", Lecture XIII: 39.

come into my garden'" [Song 5:1]. "Now in the place where He was crucified was a garden" [John 19:41] . . . The Tree of life therefore was planted in the earth, that the earth which had been cursed might enjoy the blessing, and that the dead might be released.[13]

Standing in the shadow of Mount Calvary, Cyril celebrates the Cross as a Tree of new Life inaugurating a new creation, a new beginning for humanity, a fresh start in which Christ's obedience and forgiveness unbinds for all time Adam's disobedience and sin.

Echoing the words associated with Constantine at his vision of the Cross—"In this sign conquer"—Cyril exhorts us to practice making the sign of the Cross in different situations, in order to claim its victory:

> Let us not then be ashamed to confess the Crucified. Let the Cross be our seal made with boldness by our fingers in our brow, and on everything; over the bread we eat, and the cups we drink; in our comings in, and goings out; before our sleep, when we lie down and when we rise up; when we are in the way, and when we are still. Great is that preservative; it is without price, for the sake of the poor; without toil, for the sick; since also its grace is from God. It is the Sign of the faithful, and the dread of devils: for "He triumphed over them in it, having made a show of them openly" [Col 2:15]; for when they see the Cross they are reminded of the Crucified; they are afraid of Him, who bruised the heads of the dragon [Ps 74:13]. Do not despise the Seal, because of the freeness of the gift; out of this rather honor your Benefactor.[14]

Those hearing Cyril's voice for the first time, the catechumens in training, will appropriate all this in their forthcoming Baptism: soon, indeed, they will receive the sacred seal of the Cross in the initiation rite made with the holy chrism on forehead, ears, nostrils, breast.[15] Cyril exhorts them to a steadfast confession of the Cross in time of trial:

> You see this spot of Golgotha! You answer with a shout of praise, as if assenting. See that you recant not in time of persecution. Rejoice not in the Cross in time of peace only. But hold fast the same faith in time of persecution also; be not in peace a friend of Jesus, and His foe in times of wars. You receive now remission of your sins, and the gifts of the King's spiritual bounty; when war shall come strive nobly for your King. Jesus, the Sinless, was crucified for you;

13. Gifford, "Cyril of Jerusalem", Lecture XIII: 118, 19, 31, 32, 35.
14. Gifford, "Cyril of Jerusalem", Lecture XIII: 36.
15. Gifford, "Cyril of Jerusalem", Lecture XXI.

and will not you be crucified for Him who was crucified for you? You are not bestowing a favor, for you have first received, but you are returning a favor, repaying your debt to Him who was crucified for you in Golgotha.[16]

HESYCHIUS THE PRESBYTER (d.450), takes up this challenge in a powerful sermon preached in the Church of the Resurrection adjoining Mount Calvary a hundred years later in 448. Hesychius is virtually unknown in the West but renowned in the Eastern Church as a monk, theologian, biblical commentator, and brilliant scholar. A native of Jerusalem and a student of Gregory Nazianzus, after the death of his mentor, he settled in the Judean desert. In the year 412, the Bishop of Jerusalem ordained Hesychius as a presbyter. Many of Hesychius' writings have been lost, though scholars continue to identify more of his works hidden among Greek manuscripts and Latin translations: some are still buried in libraries, yet undiscovered.[17] The Greek Menology (service book) states that Hesychius made an exposition of the entire Scriptures. His extant biblical commentaries include interpretations of Leviticus, Job, Isaiah, and Ezekiel, containing many geographical and topographical allusions to the holy places of Palestine.[18] His hermeneutical approach followed Origen's allegorical method, with a highly symbolic reading of the text.

On the occasion of the memorial of Procopius of Caesarea who had been martyred under the emperor Diocletian in 303 Hesychius preached a memorable sermon. Though it seemed that the age of persecutions had passed, Hesychius, inspired by the message of Calvary, exhorts his hearers not to be faint-hearted:

> Exercise moderation. Bring about justice. Train yourself in patience... pursue humility... Don't resile from trials, for "happy is the man who endures trials" [Jas 1:12]. Don't demand exemptions from persecutions, since "blessed are those who are persecuted for justice's sake, because theirs is the kingdom of heaven" [Matt 5:10]. Don't avoid danger, for "the dangers of Hades have found me, and I have called on the name of the Lord" [Ps 114:3–4] says David, and like an ally he has come from heaven to meet me. Don't be timid in the face of death, for just now you heard the church

---

16. Gifford, "Cyril of Jerusalem", Lecture XIII:23.

17. Appended to the "Legend of the Martyrdom of St. Longinus" (Migne, *Patrologia Graeca 93*, 545–60) is the testimony of "Hesychius Presbyter of Jerusalem" himself, that he had discovered the manuscript in the library of the Holy Sepulcher.

18. Migne, *Patrologia Graeca* 93,787–1560.

> singing: "Precious before the Lord is the death of his saints" [Ps 115:6] and this is quite proper...
> Whether tribulation lays siege to the human being, whether distress constrains the believer . . . whether dangers encircle him, whether the sword has been sharpened, none of these things could separate the believer from Christ, none could set the soldier apart from his king. I mean that if tribulation lays siege to them, on seeing Christ, the prince of joy, they rejoice; if distress constrains them, on looking at the teacher they relax; if persecution dogs them, on looking forward to heaven they take no thought for earth, but steady their feet in order not to stumble...

Referring to the context of his preaching, the Church of the Resurrection close by Calvary, Hesychius concludes his sermon:

> Direct your gaze with zeal toward this royal Cross, contemplate it and, after it, consider this holy temple, the Resurrection. Draw for yourself the king hanging on a tree, a master wrongly beaten by slaves [Matt 26:67], a lawgiver shamelessly spat upon by subordinates [Matt 26:67], the one who is opulent in all his clothes imprudently stripped of his tunic [Matt 26:28]. But look, do you see the Resurrection in all these events? In this spot, the linen cloths of the one who was stripped prove his wealth, angels will demonstrate the power of the one who was beaten, the voices of those who came down from heaven reveal the glory of the one who was slapped. To him be the glory now and always and forever and ever. Amen. [19]

Living and working on Mount Calvary Hesychius long pondered the significance of the crucifixion and resurrection. His *Easter Homily* exults in the reality of the risen life...

> The teaching of scripture is that he must rise from the dead.
> The festival we celebrate today, is one of victory—the victory of the son of God, king of the whole universe. On this day the devil is defeated by the crucified one; our race is filled with joy by the risen one. In honor of my resurrection in Christ this day cries out:
> "In my journey I beheld a new wonder—an open tomb, a man risen from the dead, bones exulting, souls rejoicing, men and women refashioned, the heavens opened, and powers crying out: 'Lift up your gates, you princes; be lifted up, you everlasting doors, that the king of glory may come in.'

19. "Hesychius of Jerusalem: A homily in praise of Saint Procopius" in Leemans, *Greek Homilies*, 208–10, 212–13.

Calvary

"On this day I saw the king of heaven, robed in light, ascend above the lightning and the rays of the sun, above the sun and the sources of water, above the dwelling place of the angelic powers and the city of eternal life."

Hidden first in a womb of flesh, he sanctified human birth by his own birth; hidden afterward in the womb of the earth, he gave life to the dead by his Resurrection. Suffering, pain, and sighs have now fled away.

For who has known the mind of God, or who has been his counselor if not the Word made flesh, who was nailed to the Cross, who rose from the dead, and who was taken up into heaven?

This day brings a message of joy: it is the day of the Lord's Resurrection when, with himself, he raised up the race of Adam. Born for the sake of human beings, he rose from the dead with them.

On this day paradise is opened by the risen one, Adam is restored to life and Eve is consoled.

On this day the divine call is heard, the kingdom is prepared, we are saved and Christ is adored.

On this day, when he had trampled death under foot, made the tyrant a prisoner, and despoiled the underworld, Christ ascended into heaven as a king in victory, as a ruler in glory, as an invincible charioteer.

He said to the Father: "here am I, O God, with the children you have given me" and he heard the Father's reply: "Sit at my right hand until I make your enemies your footstool." To him be glory, now and for ever, through endless ages, Amen.[20]

SOPHRONIUS (560–638), Patriarch of Jerusalem, celebrates the wonder of Mount Calvary. At the Arab conquest of the holy city, Sophronius met the Caliph Omar at the Church of the Resurrection, and indeed invited him to pray there. The Caliph declined, saying that such an action would require the church to become a mosque. He is credited with agreeing in 637 the so-called Covenant of Omar with the existing residents of Jerusalem preserving their rights of worship. This moving poem *Anacreonticon* 20, written in 614 when Sophronius was absent from the city, reveals the depths of his passion for the holy places associated with the death and resurrection of Jesus:

---

20. Hesychius, *Easter Homily*, 66–69.

Voices from the Mountains

Holy City of God,
Jerusalem, how I long to stand
Even now at your gates, and go in, rejoicing!
A divine longing for holy Sion
Presses upon me insistently.

[Church of the Resurrection]
Let me walk thy pavements
and go inside the *Anastasis*,
where the King of All rose again,
trampling down the power of death . . .

Through the divine sanctuary
I will penetrate the divine Tomb,
and with deep reverence
will venerate that Rock.

And as I venerate that worthy Tomb,
surrounded by its conches
and columns surmounted by golden lilies,
I shall be overcome with joy.

[Rock of the Cross]
Let me pass on to the sacred court,
all covered with pearls and gold,
and go on into the lovely building
of the Place of a Skull.

Ocean of life ever living
and of the true oblivion.
Tomb that gives light!

And prostrate I will venerate
the Navel-point of the earth, that divine Rock
in which was fixed the wood
which undid the curse of the tree.

How great thy glory,
noble Rock, in which was fixed
the Cross, the Redemption of mankind!

Exultant let me go on to the place
where all of us
who belong to the people of God
venerate the glorious Wood of the Cross.

Let me run to bend the knee
before the artist's picture
representing the Rulers,
to render homage.

[Constantinian Basilica of the Martyrium]
And let me go rejoicing
to the splendid sanctuary, the place
where the noble Empress Helena
found the divine Wood;

and go up,
my heart overcome with awe,
and see the Upper Room,
the Reed, the Sponge, and the Lance.

Then may I gaze down
upon the fresh beauty of the Basilica
where choirs of monks
sing nightly songs of worship.[21]

QUESTIONS FOR TODAY

We find ourselves living in a time of uncertainty, when many are faint-hearted and fearful. The voices from Calvary and the empty tomb infuse us with courage. Cyril preparing new Christians for the life of faith ahead of them, and Hesychius preaching to pilgrims, put new heart into their hearers—and this, of course, is the very meaning of "courage", from Latin *cor* "heart." Their words challenge the disheartened, and encourage those that are scarred and scared.

Cyril says: "Rejoice not in the Cross in time of peace only. But hold fast the same faith in time of persecution also; be not in peace a friend of Jesus, and His foe in times of wars." As we look to Mount Calvary, we see the courage of Jesus who faces suffering and death—he does not run away.

---

21. Wilkinson, *Jerusalem Pilgrims*, 157–58.

He had, indeed, faced that temptation in Gethsemane ("Let this cup pass from me") but now he is ready to drink its dregs.

When we look at the Cross we see God's solidarity with all who suffer. And when we look at the Cross we see the paradox of victory in seeming defeat, the promise of life in the midst of death. As a sixth century hymn puts it:

> Sing, my tongue the glorious battle, sing the ending of the fray.
> Now above the Cross, the trophy, sound the loud triumphant lay:
> Tell how Christ, the world's redeemer as a victim won the day.
>
> Faithful Cross, true sign of triumph, be for all the noblest tree;
> None in foliage, none in blossom, none in fruit your equal be;
> Symbol of the world's redemption, for the weight that hung on thee.[22]

Hesychius calls us to hold on tightly to the Easter reality:

> This day brings a message of joy: it is the day of the Lord's Resurrection when, with himself, he raised up the race of Adam. Born for the sake of human beings, he rose from the dead with them.
> On this day paradise is opened by the risen one, Adam is restored to life and Eve is consoled.
> On this day the divine call is heard, the kingdom is prepared, we are saved and Christ is adored.

"The divine call is heard": Hesychius reminds us that the empty tomb calls us to walk in newness of life, to walk with heads held up high, for he is clear:

> Don't resile from trials . . .
> Don't avoid danger . . .
> Don't be timid in the face of death . . .
> Whether tribulation lays siege to the human being, whether distress constrains the believer . . . whether dangers encircle him, whether the sword has been sharpened, none of these things could separate the believer from Christ, none could set the soldier apart from his king.

Mount Cavalry is a mountain of deepest pain and greatest hope. The site of the crucifixion, with its rocky limestone cliff still visible within the Church of the Holy Sepulcher, stands very close indeed to the empty tomb, preserved for pilgrims to this day. On this sacred mount the very site tells

---

22. Venantius Honorius Clematianus Fortunatus (530- 609), *Sing my tongue, the glorious battle* translated by John Mason Neale.

Calvary

us that suffering and hope are intertwined, that pain and deliverance are close by to each other: "Now there was a garden in the place where he was crucified, and in the garden there was a new tomb" (John 19:41).

Hearing the voices of Cyril, Hesychius and Sophronius from this cosmic mountain, let us then take heart and make our own the prayer: "Lord Jesus, as this day begins we remember that you are risen—and therefore we look to the future with confidence."[23]

"In this sign conquer!" What would your life be like if you lived according to this maxim?

FOR PERSONAL REFLECTION

1. Both Cyril and Hesychius, at the very site of Calvary, call their hearers to courage and steadfastness in the face of trials. How do you find yourself responding to such calls? In what ways can the Cross fortify and hearten you in your present situation?

2. Cyril's voice calls out to us across the centuries: "Let us not then be ashamed to confess the Crucified." In what ways can you confess the Cross by your lifestyle, actions and reactions?

3. Hesychius asks of the events of Christ's sufferings: "But look, do you see the Resurrection in all these events?" Can you see signs of hope amidst trials, or clues or hints about the presence of God in the midst of circumstances where God seems absent?

4. What advice or counsel from Mount Calvary would you give to new Christians?

5. What poem or prayer can you compose in praise of Mount Calvary? Let this inspire you:

> O Cross of Christ, immortal tree on which our Savior died.
> The world is sheltered by your arms that bore the Crucified.
> Faithful Cross, you stand unmoved while ages run their course.
> Foundation of the universe, Creation's binding force.
> Give glory to the risen Christ and to his Cross give praise.
> The sign of God's unfathomed love, the hope of all our days.[24]

---

23. "Morning Prayer for Tuesday Week 2", *The Divine Office*, 490.
24. Stanbrook Abbey, used with permission.

Conclusion

Forgetting what lies behind, and straining forward to what lies ahead, I press on toward the goal (Phil 3:13,14)

Is our journey complete, now we have ascended the biblical mounts? We have only just begun! We turn again to Gregory of Nyssa, one of the outstanding theologians of the Eastern Church, whom we met at Sinai. We recall he saw the Exodus journey as a prefiguration of the Christian's pilgrimage of faith. He cries out to us across the centuries: "No limit can interrupt growth in the ascent to God!"[1] He communicates an exciting vision of the spiritual life as continually evolving and progressing, energized by the Holy Spirit. His key text is the resolve of Paul: "Forgetting what lies behind, and straining forward to what lies ahead, I press on toward the goal, for the prize of the upward call of God in Christ Jesus" (Phil 3:13–14). Paul is saying that there is no room for self-satisfaction in the Christian life. We should never stand still, but continually stretch ourselves towards the "upward call."

God invites us to make Christian vocation an adventure, in which we are beckoned to keep on moving. Gregory urges us to break free from any

---

1. Gregory of Nyssa, *Life of Moses*, 116.

way of life that seems deterministic and predictable; to jump off the treadmill of dull routine which traps us into going round in circles. Rather he encourages us to discover our full potential in Christ:

> The finest aspect of our mutability is the possibility of growth in good . . . let us change in such a way that we may constantly evolve towards what is better, being transformed from glory into glory, and thus always improving and ever becoming more perfect by daily growth.[2]

For Gregory, each stage reached in the spiritual journey is but a beginning, not an end. Pilgrims can never say they have arrived. As the letter to the Hebrews puts it: "Let us lay aside every weight, and sin which clings so closely, and let us run with perseverance the race that is set before us, looking to Jesus the pioneer and perfecter of our faith" (Heb 12:1). In Gregory's eyes, the greatest sin is that of complacency, of resting on one's laurels. Gregory's vision is one of lifelong-learning or rather, eternal progress—he calls it *epekstasis*, reaching out. As Malherbe and Ferguson put it: "There is an incessant transformation into the likeness of God as one stretches out with the divine infinity; there is an ever-greater participation in God."[3] In *The Life of Moses*, each new summit the patriarch conquers is but an invitation to see wider horizons and higher ascents to be made. When you reach the summit of one mountain, there is no need for a sense of self-congratulation—it just enables you to see the other mounts, near and far on the horizon, that beckon you next!

Gregory develops this idea as he sees in *The Song of Songs* a powerful allegory of the relationship between God (the bridegroom) and the seeker (the bride). The Bridegroom is a dynamic figure, ever in movement: "Behold, he comes, leaping upon the mountains, bounding over the hills. My beloved is like a gazelle" (Song 2:8,9). What is his message to his bride as she relaxes and rests on her couch? "My beloved speaks and says to me, 'Arise, my love, my fair one, and come away . . .'" (2:3). He repeats this call again (2:10). Gregory comments:

> For this reason the Word says once again to his awakened Bride: *Arise*; and when she has come, *Come*. For he who is rising can always rise further, and for him who runs to the Lord the open field of the divine course is never exhausted. We must therefore

---

2. Musurillo, *From Glory to Glory*, 51–52.
3. Gregory of Nyssa, *Life of Moses*, 12.

> constantly arouse ourselves . . . for as often as He says *Arise* and
> *Come*, He gives us the power to rise and make progress.[4]

In this image, Gregory sees a powerful metaphor of our vocation. We are not to allow ourselves to become too content with where we are spiritually. We are not to rest in our achievements. God ever calls us to the next stage of our development. Every point of arrival is to be a spring-board that catapults us into another adventure! We must keep moving. As Gregory observes: Moses "always found a step higher than the one he had attained."[5]

This however requires of us great determination and resolve. We need to foster an unending sense of yearning and desire to grow in faith. For Gregory, it is a question of a partnership between human effort and divine help. It is the Holy Spirit who can transform our vocation into an adventure of moving further into the mystery of God. He enables us to participate in the divine life itself, which animates, vivifies and completes human life:

> The rich and ungrudging Spirit is always flowing into those accepting grace . . . for those who have taken possession of this gift sincerely, it endures as a co-worker and companion in accordance with the measure of faith.[6]

The Holy Spirit helps us reach our full potential and an ever-increasing likeness to God; as Gregory puts it: "The soul having been brought to the full flower of its beauty by the grace of the Spirit."[7] Gregory pictures the Holy Spirit as a Dove who not only broods over our life, but actually gives us wings to fly, never staying put for long upon the mountain, but ever ascending : "the soul keeps rising higher and higher, stretching with its desire for heavenly things 'to those that are before' as the Apostle tells us, and thus it will always continue to soar ever higher."[8]

If we are to be guided and directed by the Spirit, what part is there for human effort? Gregory is emphatic:

> Do not acquiesce in His gifts, thinking that because of the wealth and ungrudging grace of the Spirit nothing else is needed for perfection . . . It is necessary, then, never to relax the tension of toil or stand aside from the struggles at hand or turn to the past

---

4. Musurillo, *From Glory to Glory*, 191.
5. Gregory of Nyssa, *Life of Moses*, 114.
6. Gregory of Nyssa, *Ascetical Works*, 129.
7. Gregory of Nyssa, *Ascetical Works*, 130.
8. Musurillo, *From Glory to Glory*, 57.

Conclusion

if something good has been accomplished, but to forget "what is behind" (Phil 3:13) and look to the future.⁹

Gregory is encouraging us to work closely with the Spirit in a *synergy* or close co-operation. The adventure of continual growth is, in a sense, an abiding struggle, but Gregory assures us: "always nurtured by the grace of the Spirit and taking power from Christ, we may easily run the course of salvation, making light and pleasant the struggle . . . with God Himself assisting us in our eagerness."¹⁰

Gregory's perspective is especially helpful at this time. As we review recent challenging months, we can permit ourselves to celebrate breakthroughs, triumphs and any creative shifts in our thinking—in a spirit of thanksgiving for any blessings, not one of self-congratulation. Circumstances beyond our control have actually given us the opportunity to grow in some ways—we may never be the same again. As we emerge from a time of pandemic we should not long with nostalgia for a world that is passed but embrace the new future and help build a kinder, gentler world, in partnership with the divine Spirit. There are more mountains to climb and explore, and more voices to be heard!

OUR JOURNEY IN THIS BOOK

We have indeed heard some remarkable voices addressing us and speaking into our present situation. In the shadow of Ararat, Gregory of Narek and Nerses Shnorhali called us to take another look at our understanding of the vocation of the church in turbulent times and reflect on our image of God. On Sinai, John Climacus, Hesychios and Philotheos called us to watchfulness, alertness to the Divine and showed us that we can find God in the deepest darkness. On Mount Carmel Albert and John of the Cross summoned us to reflect on our dual vocation to be mystics and prophets for a troubled world.

On Mount Zion the longing of our own soul found an echo in the deep thirst for God expressed in the voices of Moses Maimonides and Yehuda Halevi; Raba'a and Al-Ghazali; Sophronius and Bernard of Clairvaux. Clambering amongst the rocks of the Judean desert we caught the whispers of the earliest monks Chariton and Euthymius and we found that their

---

9. Gregory of Nyssa, *Ascetical Works*, 141,144.
10. Gregory of Nyssa, *Ascetical Works*, 151.

cries strangely resonated with contemporary concerns. Jerome helped us to climb the Galilean mountains and hear afresh their message. On awesome Mount Tabor we listened to Gregory Palamas and encountered a different take on the Transfiguration story, realizing that we could change too, not least in our powers of perception. Remarkable women heartened and challenged us atop Olivet—the two indomitable Melanias, with Rufinus in their shadow, showed us how we can regain hopefulness in an uncertain world and see visions through to fulfilment. On the sacred hill of Calvary, Cyril and Hesychius of Jerusalem beckoned us to new courage and steadfastness in the face of trials. I trust that these voices have heartened, challenged and inspired you in your ongoing spiritual adventure.

Let us conclude by celebrating with Isaiah the potential of the mountains—because for him, the mountains are not only a place of discovery and learning. For him, and for us too, justice, peace and wisdom go out from the holy mountain to transform the world:

> In days to come the mountain of the LORD's house
> shall be established as the highest of the mountains,
>   and shall be raised above the hills;
> all the nations shall stream to it.
>   Many peoples shall come and say,
> "Come, let us go up to the mountain of the LORD,
>   to the house of the God of Jacob;
> that he may teach us his ways
>   and that we may walk in his paths."
> For out of Zion shall go forth instruction,
>   and the word of the LORD from Jerusalem.
> He shall judge between the nations,
>   and shall arbitrate for many peoples;
> they shall beat their swords into plowshares,
>   and their spears into pruning hooks;
> nation shall not lift up sword against nation,
>   neither shall they learn war any more.
> O house of Jacob,
> come, let us walk
> in the light of the LORD! (Isa 2:2–5)

Conclusion

FOR PERSONAL REFLECTION

1. As you review the journey of this book, which is the most memorable mountain you have climbed? Why?
2. Which voice has startled you or surprised you?
3. Which voice have you found the most challenging to you in your situation?
4. How might you act or think differently as a result of hearing that voice?
5. How do you find yourself responding to Gregory's vision of continual growth and movement within your own evolving and unfolding vocation?

Bibliography

Alson, William P. *Perceiving God: the Epistemology of Religious Experience*. Ithaca and London: Cornell University Press, 1991.
Aubineau, Michel, ed. *Homélies Pascales: Hésychius de Jérusalem, Basile de Séleucie, Jean de Béryte, Pseudo-Chrysostome, Léonce de Constantinople*. Paris: Éditions du Cerf, Sources Chrétiennes 187, 1972.
Barber, Malcolm and Bate, Keith, trans. *The Templars: Selected Sources Translated and Annotated*. Manchester: Manchester University Press, 2002.
Barrois, Georges, trans. *The Fathers Speak*. New York: St Vladimir's Seminary, 1986.
Barreau, Jean-Claude. "Preface." In Oliver Clement, *The Roots of Christian Mysticism*, 7-8. London: New City, 1993.
Benedict, Abbot of Monte Cassino. *The Rule of St Benedict in English*. Translated by Timothy Fry. Collegeville, Minnesota: Liturgical, 1982.
Bessant, Walter. "The Holy Sepulcher." In *Dictionary of Christian Antiquities*, edited by William Smith and Samuel Cheetham. Hartford: J.B. Burr, 1880.
Biddle, Martin, Avni G. et al, *The Church of the Holy Sepulcher*. New York: Rizzoli, 2000.
Binns, John. *Ascetics and Ambassadors of Christ: The Monasteries of Palestine, 314-631*. Oxford: Clarendon, 1994.
Boff, Leonardo. *Jesus Christ Liberator: A Critical Christology For Our Times*. New York: Orbis, 1978.
Borg, Marcus J. *Jesus: A New Vision*. San Francisco: Harper, 1992.
Brundell, Michael. "Themes in Carmelite Spiritual Direction." In *Traditions of Spiritual Guidance* edited by Lavinia Byrne, 64-77. Collegeville, Minnesota: Liturgical, 1990.
Bryant, Christopher. *Journey to the Centre*. London: Darton, Longman and Todd, 1987.
Cameron, Averil and Hall, Stuart G., trans. *Eusebius' Life of Constantine: Introduction, Translation, and Commentary*. Oxford: Clarendon, 1999.
Casaldaliga, Pedro and Vigil, Jose Maria. *The Spirituality of Liberation*. Tunbridge Wells: Burns and Oates,1994.

Bibliography

Chilton, Bruce. *Rabbi Jesus*. London: Image/ Doubleday, 2002.
Chitty, Derwas. *The Desert A City: An Introduction to the Study of Egyptian and Palestinian Monasticism Under the Christian Empire*. New York: St Vladimir's Seminary, 1997.
Clark, Elizabeth A., trans. *The Life of Melania the Younger*. New York: Edwin Mellen, 1984.
Clifford, Richard J. *The Cosmic Mountain in Canaan and the Old Testament*. Eugene, OR: Wipf and Stock, 2010.
Climacus, John. *The Ladder of Divine Ascent*. Translated by Colm Luibheid and Norman Russell. New York: Paulist, 1982.
———. *The Ladder of Divine Ascent*. Translated by Lazarus Moore. Boston, Mass: Holy Transfiguration Monastery, 1978.
Cohick, Lynn H. and Hughes, Amy Brown. *Christian Women in the Patristic World: their Influence, Authority and Legacy in the Second through Fifth Centuries*. Grand Rapids, Michigan: Baker Academic, 2017.
Cullmann, Oscar. *Prayer in the New Testament*. London: SCM, 1995.
Davidson, Herbert A. *Moses Maimonides: The Man and His Works*. Oxford: Oxford University Press 2010.
Cyril of Scythopolis. *Lives of the Monks of Palestine*. Translated by R. M. Rice. Kalamazoo, Michigan: Cistercian, 1991.
Daley, Brian E., trans. *Light on the Mountain: Greek Patristic and Byzantine Homilies on the Transfiguration of the Lord*. New York: St. Vladimir's Seminary, 2013.
Donaldson, Terence L. *Jesus on the Mountain: A Study in Matthean Theology*. Sheffield: JSOT, 1985.
Dunn, James D.G. *Jesus Remembered*. Michigan: Eerdmans, 2003.
Edwards, Bede, trans. "The Rule of St Albert." In Obbard, Elizabeth Ruth, *Land of Carmel*, 39–44. Leominster: Gracewing, 1999.
Episcopal Conferences of England and Wales. *Morning and Evening Prayer from The Divine Office*. Glasgow: William Collins Sons and Co, 1976.
Evagrius of Pontus. *The Praktis, Chapters on Prayer*. Translated by John Eudes Bamberger. Trappist, Kentucky: Cistercian, 1972.
———. *Letter to Melania*. Translated by Martin Parmentier. Utrecht: [publisher not identified], 1985.
———. *Letter to Melania*. Translated by Luke Dysinger. http://www.ldysinger.com/Evagrius/11_Letters/64_great_letter_to_melania.htm
Follent, John. "Negative Experience and Christian Growth." In *St John of the Cross*, edited by Peter Slattery, 83–100. New York: Alba House, 1994.
Foster, Richard. *Celebration of Discipline: The Path to Spiritual Growth*. London: Hodder and Stoughton, 1980.
Francis, Pope. *Let us Dream: The Path to a Better Future*. New York: Simon & Schuster, 2020.
Freemantle, W. M., trans. *The Life and Works of Rufinus, with Jerome's Apology Against Rufinus*. London: Aeterna, 2016. Also available at https://www.newadvent.org/fathers/2711.htm
van Gennep, Arnold. *Rites de Passage*. London: Routledge, 2010.
Al-Ghazali. *Deliverance from Error*. Translated by Richard J. McCarthy. Boston: Fons Vitae, 2001.
———. *Love, Longing and Contentment—Book XXXVI of The Revival of the Religious Sciences*. Translated by Eric Ormsby. Cambridge: The Islamic Texts Society, 2011.

Bibliography

Frenkel, Miriam. "The Temple Mount in Jewish Thought (70CE to the Present)." In *Where Heaven and Earth Meet: Jerusalem's Sacred Esplanade*, edited by Oleg Grabar and Benjamin Z. Kedar, 344–261. Jerusalem: Yad Ben-Zvi, 2009.

Freyne, Sean. *Galilee, Jesus and the Gospels: Literary Approaches and Historical Investigations*. Philadelphia: Fortress, 1988.

———. *Jesus, A Jewish Galilean: a new reading of the Jesus-story*. London: T & T Clark, 2004.

Gifford, Edwin H., trans., "The Catechetical Lectures of Cyril of Jerusalem." In *A Select Library of Nicene and Post-Nicene Fathers of the Christian Church Series II, Vol VII*, edited by Philip Schaff and Henry Wace. New York: Christian Literature Company, 1893.

Gingras, George E., trans. *Egeria: Diary of a Pilgrimage*. New York: Newman, 1970.

Gregory of Narek. *Speaking with God from the Depths of the Heart*. Translated by Thomas J. Samuelian. Yerevan: Vem, 2002.

Gregory of Nyssa: *The Life of Moses*. Translated by Abraham J. Malherbe and Everett Ferguson. New York: Paulist, 1978.

———. *Ascetical Works (The Fathers of the Church)*. Translated by Virginia Woods Callahan. Washington: Catholic University of America Press, 1967.

Halkin, Hillel, trans., *Yehuda Halevi*. New York: Schocken, 2010. https://www.tabletmag.com/sections/news/articles/zion-do-you-wonder.

Helminski, Camille Adams. *Women of Sufism: A Hidden Treasure*. Boston and London: Shambhala, 2003.

Hesychius of Jerusalem, *Easter Homily*. Source Chrétiennes 187: 66–69. https://liturgy.slu.edu/Triduum2020A/theword_journey.html

Hilkins, Andy. "An Armenian Invocational Prayer." *Hugoye: Journal of Syriac Studies* 23 (2020) 264–73. https://hugoye.bethmardutho.org/article/hv23n2hilkens.

Hirschfeld, Yizhar. *Judean Desert Monasteries in the Byzantine Period*. Yale University Press, 1992.

Holmes, Augustine. *A Life Pleasing to God: The Spirituality of the Rules of St Basil*. London: Darton, Longman and Todd 2000.

Horsley, Richard A. *Archaeology, History and Society in Galilee: The Social Context of Jesus and the Rabbis*. Valley Forge: Trinity International, 1995.

Jerome. *Commentary on Matthew*. Translated by Thomas P. Scheck. Washington DC: Catholic University of America Press, 2008.

John of the Cross. *The Collected Works*. Translated by Kieran Kavanaugh and Otilio Rodriguez. Washington: ICS, 1991.

Jones, Cheslyn. "Mysticism, human and divine." In *The Study of Spirituality* edited by C. P.M, Jones, et al, 17–23. London: SPCK, 1986.

Lane, Belden C. *The Solace of Fierce Landscapes*. Oxford: Oxford University Press, 1998.

Lee, Sang H. *From a Liminal Place: an Asian American Theology*. Minneapolis: Fortress, 2010.

Leemans, Johan et al, trans. *'Let us Die That We May Live': Greek Homilies on Christian Martyrs from Asia Minor, Palestine and Syria (c.350–450AD)*. London: Routledge, 2003.

Lossky, Vladimir. *The Mystical Theology of the Eastern Church*. London: James Clarke and Co. Ltd., 1957.

———. *In the image and likeness of God*. Oxford: Mowbrays, 1975.

Louth, Andrew. *The Origins of the Christian Mystical Tradition*. Oxford: University Press, 1981.

Bibliography

———. *Denys the Aeropagite*. New York: Continuum, 1989.
———. "Theology, Contemplation and the University", *Studia Theologica* I:2 (2003) 64–73.
Macquarrie, John. *Paths in Spirituality*. London: SCM, 1972.
Maimonides, Moses. *Guide for the Perplexed*. Translated by M. Friedländer. Pantianos Classics, reprint of 1910 edition. Also at sacred-texts.com
Maloney, George A. *Intoxicated with God: the Fifty Spiritual Homilies of Macarius*. New Jersey: Dimension,1978.
Mayes, Andrew D. *Holy Land? Challenging Questions from the Biblical Landscape*. London: SPCK, 2011.
———. *Another Christ: re-envisioning ministry*. London: SPCK, 2014.
———. *Gateways to the Divine: transformative pathways of prayer from the Holy City of Jerusalem*. Eugene, Oregon: Cascade, 2020.
———. *Journey to the Centre of the Soul*. Abingdon: BRF, 2017.
Matthews, Melvyn. *Both Alike to Thee: The Retrieval of the Mystical Way*. London: SPCK, 2000.
McAfee Brown, Robert. *Spirituality and Liberation: Overcoming the Great Fallacy*. London: Hodder and Stoughton, 1988.
McGinn, Bernard. *The Foundation of Mysticism: Vol. I: Origins to the 5th Century*. London: SCM, 1991.
McKenna, Paul. "Mind Tricks to Beat Stress." London: Daily Mail, 16 January 2021.
Merton, Thomas. *The Wisdom of the Desert*. Boston and London, Shambhala, 1960.
Meyendorff, Jean, *St. Gregory Palamas and Orthodox Spirituality*. New York: St Vladimir's Seminary,1974.
———. *Byzantine Theology: Historical Trends and Doctrinal Themes*. Oxford: Mowbray, 1975.
Migne, Jacques-Paul. *Patrologia Graeca 40: SS. Patrum Aegyptiorum*. Paris: Migne, 1863.
———. *Patrologia Graeca 46: S.P.N. Gregorii, Episcopi Nysseni*. Turnhout, Belgium: Brepols [no date]
———. *Patrologia Graeca 93: SS. Patrum, doctorum scriptorumque ecclesiasticorum*. Turnhout, Belgium: Brepols, 1956.
———. *Patrologia Latina 29: Sancti Hieronymi*. Paris: Migne, 1846.
Miles, Margaret R. *The Image and Practice of Holiness*. London: SCM, 1988.
Moltmann, Jurgen. *The Spirit of Life: A Universal Affirmation*. London: SCM, 1992.
Murphy, Francis X., "Melania the Elder: A Biographical Note", *Traditio* Vol. 5. Cambridge University Press, 1947.
Musurillo, Herbert. trans. *From Glory to Glory: Texts from Gregory of Nyssa's Mystical Writings*. London: John Murray, 1962.
Myrie, Clive. "Royal London Hospital Reports 18 January 2021." https://www.bbc.co.uk/news/av/health-55708709
Nasr, Seyyed Hossein. *Islamic Spirituality: Manifestations*. London: SCM, 1991.
Need, Stephen. *Jerusalem: Church of the Holy Sepulchre*. Jerusalem: Carta, 2016.
———. *Following Jesus in the Holy Land*. Durham: Sacristy, 2019.
Newman, Hillel I. "Between Jerusalem and Bethlehem: Jerome and the holy places of Palestine." In *Sanctity of Time and Space in Tradition and Modernity*, edited by A. Houtman et al, 220–225. Leiden: Brill,1998.
Nicholson, Reynold A. *The Mystics of Islam*. Beirut: Khayats, 1966.
Nouwen, Henri. *The Way of the Heart: Desert Spirituality and Contemporary Ministry*. London: Darton, Longman and Todd, 1987.

Bibliography

Palamas Gregory. *The Triads*. Translated by Nicholas Gendle. New York: Paulist, 1983.

———. "Homily on the Transfiguration." https://orthochristian.com/38767.html

Palmer, George E.H. et al., trans. *The Philokalia, Vol 1*. London: Faber and Faber,1979; Vol 2 1981, Vol 3 1986.

Palladius, *Historia Lausiaca*. Translated by Cuthbert Butler. Cambridge: Cambridge University Press 1904, repr. Hildesheim: Georg Olms, 1967.

———. *Lausiac History*. Translated by Robert T. Meyer. New York: Paulist, Ancient Christian Writers, 1964.

Petersen, Joan. *Handmaids of the Lord: Contemporary Descriptions of Feminine Asceticism in the First Six Christian Centuries*. Collegeville, Minnesota: Cistercian, 1996.

Powell, Mark A. *The Jesus Debate: Modern Historians Investigate the Life of Christ*. Oxford: Lion, 1998.

Pseudo-Dionysius. *The Complete Works*. Translated by Colm Luibheid. New York: Paulist, 1987.

Rahner, Karl. *Theological Investigations 20*. New York: Crossroads, 1981.

Rampolla del Tindaro. *The Life of St Melania*. Translated by E. Leahy. London: Burns and Oates, 1905.

Renard, John. *Knowledge of God in Classical Sufism: Foundations of Islamic Mystical Theology*. New York: Paulist, 2004.

Rohr, Richard. *Naked Now: Learning to See as the Mystics See*. New York: Crossroad, 2009.

Sanders, E.P. *The Historical Figure of Jesus*. London: Penguin, 1993.

Scheindlin, Raymond P. *The Song of the Distant Dove: Judah Halevi's Pilgrimage*. Oxford University Press, 2007.

Schroeder, Caroline T., "Exemplary Women." In *Melania: Early Christianity Through the Life of One Family*, edited by Catherine M. Chin and Caroline T. Schroeder, 50–66. Oakland, California: University of California Press, 2017.

Shedadeh, Raja. *Palestinian Walks*. London: Profile, 2008.

Sheldrake, Philip. *Spirituality and History*. London: SPCK, 1991.

Shnorhali, Nerses *Jesus, Son Only Begotten of the Father*. Translated by Jane S. Wingate, New York: Delphic, 1947.

———. *Jesus, the Son*. Translated by Mischa Kudian. London: Mashtots, 1986.

di Segni, Leah, trans. "The Life of Chariton." In *Ascetic Behavior in Greco-Roman Antiquity: A Sourcebook*, edited by Vincent L Wimbush, 393–424.Minneapolis: Fortress, 1990.

Smelt, Joachim. *The Carmelites*. Darien, IL: Carmelite Spiritual Center, 1988.

Soelle, Dorothy. *The Inward Road and the Way Back*. London: Darton, Longman and Todd, 1978.

Staniloae, Dumitru. *The Experience of God: Revelation and Knowledge of the Triune God: Orthodox Dogmatic Theology, Volume 1*. London: T and T Clark, 2000.

Swan, Laura. *The Forgotten Desert Mothers: Sayings, Lives, and Stories of Early Christian Women*. New Jersey: Paulist, 2001.

Teresa of Avila. *Interior Castle*. Translated by E. Allison Peers. London: Sheed and Ward, 1974.

———. *The Interior Castle*. Translated by Kieran Kavanaugh and Otilio Rodriguez. New York: Paulist, 1979.

Thomson, J.G.S.S. *The Praying Christ: A Study of Jesus' Doctrine and Practice of Prayer*. London: Tyndale, 1959.

Turner, Victor. *The Ritual Process: Structure and Antistructure*. Piscataway, New Jersey: Aldine Transaction, 1995.

Bibliography

Turner, V. and Turner, E. *Image and Pilgrimage in Christian Culture: anthropological perspectives*. New York: Columbia University Press, 1995.

Ulanov, Ann and Barry. *Primary Speech: A Psychology of Prayer*. Atlanta: John Knox, 1982.

Underhill, Evelyn. *Mystics of the Church*. Cambridge: James Clarke, 1925.

Upbin, Danielle. "Praying for a Rebuilt and Redeemed Jerusalem." https://www.myjewishlearning.com/article/praying-for-a-rebuilt-and-redeemed-jerusalem/

Upton, Charles, trans. *Doorkeeper of the Heart: Versions of Rabi'a*. New York: Pir, 1988.

Wallis, Jim. *The Soul of Politics*. London: Fount, 1994.

Walker, Christopher J. *Visions of Ararat: Writings on Armenia*. London: Tauris, 2005.

Ward, Benedicta, trans. *The Sayings of the Desert Fathers*. Kalamazoo: Cistercian, 1984.

Watts, Fraser and Williams, Mark. *The Psychology of Religious Knowing*. London: Chapman, 1988.

Welch, John. *The Carmelite Way*. Leominster: Gracewing, 1996.

Whitney, Donald S. *Spiritual Disciplines for the Christian Life*. Amersham, Bucks: Scripture, 1991.

Willard, Dallas. *The Spirit of the Disciplines*. San Francisco: Harper, 1991.

Williams, Rowan. *Teresa of Avila*. London: Continuum, 1991.

Wilkinson, John. *Egeria's Travels*. Oxford: Aris and Phillips, 1999.

———. *Jerusalem Pilgrims Before the Crusades*. Oxford: Aris and Phillips, 2002.

Witherington, Ben. *Jesus the Seer: The Progress of Prophecy*. Hendrickson, 1999.

Wright, N. T. *Jesus and the Victory of God*. London: SPCK, 1996.

———. *Luke for Everyone* London: SPCK, 2004.

Young, Robin Darling. "The Role of Letters in the Works of Evagrius." In *Evagrius and His Legacy*, edited by Joel Kalvesmaki and Robin Darling Young, 154–74. Notre Dame Indiana: University of Notre Dame Press, 2016.

———. "A Life in Letters." In *Melania: Early Christianity Through the Life of One Family*, edited by Catherine M. Chin and Caroline T. Schroeder, 153–70. Oakland, California: University of California Press, 2017.

www.ingramcontent.com/pod-product-compliance
Lightning Source LLC
Chambersburg PA
CBHW071449150426
43191CB00008B/1281